CHECKING for
Understanding

Formative Assessment Techniques for Your Classroom

Douglas **FISHER** | Nancy **FREY**

CHECKING for
Understanding

Formative Assessment Techniques for Your Classroom

 Association for Supervision and Curriculum Development
Alexandria, Virginia USA

ASCD®

Association for Supervision and Curriculum Development
1703 N. Beauregard St. • Alexandria, VA 22311-1714 USA
Phone: 800-933-2723 or 703-578-9600 • Fax: 703-575-5400
Web site: www.ascd.org • E-mail: member@ascd.org
Author guidelines: www.ascd.org/write

Gene R. Carter, *Executive Director;* Nancy Modrak, *Director of Publishing;* Julie Houtz, *Director of Book Editing & Production;* Leah Lakins, *Project Manager;* Greer Beeken, *Graphic Designer;* Keith Demmons, *Desktop Publishing Specialist;* Dina Murray Seamon, *Production Specialist/Team Lead*

All Web links in this book are correct as of the publication date below but may have become inactive or otherwise modified since that time. If you notice a deactivated or changed link, please e-mail books@ascd.org with the words "Link Update" in the subject line. In your message, please specify the Web link, the book title, and the page number on which the link appears.

ISBN-13: 978-1-4166-0569-0   ASCD Product #107023

ASCD Member Book, No. FY08-1 (September 2007, PC). ASCD Member Books mail to Premium (P) and Comprehensive (C) members on this schedule: Jan., PC; Feb., P; Apr., PC; May, P; July, PC; Aug., P; Sept., PC; Nov., PC; Dec., P.

Quantity discounts for the paperback edition only: 10–49 copies, 10%; 50+ copies, 15%; for 1,000 or more copies, call 800-933-2723, ext. 5634, or 703-575-5634. For desk copies: member@ascd.org.

Library of Congress Cataloging-in-Publication Data
Fisher, Douglas, 1965-
  Checking for understanding : formative assessment techniques for your classroom / Douglas Fisher and Nancy Frey.
       p. cm.
  Includes bibliographical references and index.
  ISBN 978-1-4166-0569-0 (pbk. : alk. paper) 1. Classroom management. 2. Effective teaching. I. Frey, Nancy, 1959- II. Title.

  LB3013.F515 2007
  371.27'1--dc22

                        2007015017

18 17 16 15 14 13 12 11 10 09 08 07   1 2 3 4 5 6 7 8 9 10 11 12

CHECKING for Understanding

Formative Assessment Techniques for Your Classroom

Foreword

By Jay McTighe
Educational Author and Consultant

Anyone who has ever played or coached a team sport already understands the basic idea of this book—ongoing assessment and adjustment are the *key* to improved performance. Ironically, this principle, well established in athletics and the arts, is frequently overlooked in the academic classroom. Indeed, too many teachers consider assessment as a means of obtaining grist for the grade book, instead of the process underlying progress. Of course, evaluation and grading have their place, but let's not forget the wisdom in the old farmer's quip, "You don't fatten the cattle by weighing 'em." As every effective coach understands, success in the "game," in this case, the summative assessment, begins in practice. In fact, coaching involves repeated cycles of ongoing assessment, feedback, and instruction as the primary means for improving individual and team performance. The same logic applies in the classroom.

Checking for Understanding embodies this wisdom, contending that assessment can (and should) serve academic learning, not simply as a means for measurement and evaluation. To that end, the book highlights the importance of formative, or ongoing, assessment and its role in the teaching and learning process. The research and rationale for formative assessment are clearly presented in each chapter.

Additionally, the authors offer a rich array of practical and proven methods for diagnosing students' prior knowledge and preconceptions before instruction commences and for regularly monitoring their learning along the way. A wide variety of specific examples and classroom vignettes bring the various concepts and techniques to life.

Recently, at the conclusion of an all-day workshop on the topic of assessment for learning, I asked the participants to identify one idea that they would take away from the day. One young teacher made it a point to tell me his idea: "I want to be more of a teacher on the field and more of a coach in the classroom." *Checking for Understanding* will help you do that.

P.S. Just as the book encourages teachers to regularly assess the effects of their teaching, I encourage you to actively reflect on your own assessment practices as you traverse its pages. To what extent do you use the ideas suggested? Which suggested formative assessment methods best apply to your specific teaching situation? How will you apply these ideas to enhance the learning of your students?

Introduction

We're guilty. We admit it. But we're pretty sure we're not alone.

Writing about educational practice requires that one be willing to examine one's own practice, especially the less than exemplary moments. This means admitting that we have sometimes entered into a tacit argeement with our students. We have allowed the voice of one to speak for all.

We ask, "Does everyone understand?"

We await the answer we know will come.

A lone voice says, "Yes," and we accept that as evidence that learning has occurred.

We move on to the next topic or concept, deluding ourselves that all is right with the world.

Later, much later, we review the results of the latest quiz, test, or essay, and shake our heads in wonder. "I taught all this," we say. "Didn't they get it?"

We're pretty sure we're not alone.

Breaking Our Tacit Agreements

It is said that admitting there is a problem is the first step toward change, so we hope that you've admitted—at least to yourself—that you have done the same thing. However, it's not enough to simply point out the error of your ways. We need to offer you a way to think about the situation in a new light. That means showing you how to check for understanding with your students.

This book is a tool kit. It contains a number of effective apparatuses for creating formative assessments—assessments that can be used to guide instruction and teacher decision making. Taken together and used regularly, these tools provide teachers with a system of checking for understanding. The key is to use these tools not in isolation, but as part of a system for determining what students know, what they need to know, and what types of instructional interventions are effective.

We have organized the book so that it radiates from the student's point of view. In the first chapter, we will define what checking for understanding is and is not. In addition, we will discuss some of the research on the importance of checking for understanding in promoting learning. We then invite you to take a seat at a student's desk to view learning from the user's perspective. Chapter 2 offers a discussion of checking for understanding through oral language, the most basic building block of communication in the classroom. In Chapter 3, we expand our focus on oral language to include effective questioning techniques employed by teachers who check for understanding. Chapter 4 follows with an examination of writing as another way students demonstrate what they know.

In Chapter 5, we examine how students collaborate with others on projects and performances, and how these can be used as something more than culminating activities. Chapter 6 is a detailed account of test development and analysis to check for understanding. We end with the work of teachers who collaborate to use consensus scoring to make teaching more precise.

Checking for understanding provides teachers with a set of tools necessary for the assembly of evidence that students are developing sophisticated understanding of the curriculum over time. We hope this book will serve as a tool for understanding. We have included a strategy analysis grid in the Afterword for monitoring your own learning. We have provided space for you to transfer learning to your own practice by making note of ideas for customizing the techniques in this book to your classroom, school, or district. We hope that you will discover that checking for understanding is an enduring understanding itself and that you will create new understandings between your learners and yourself.

1

Why Check for Understanding?

Checking for understanding permeates the teaching world. If you doubt that, consider the last lecture you heard. Whether the lecture was about chemical reactions, the great American novel, or the causes of World War II, the person speaking most likely checked for your understanding several times during the lecture by using such common prompts as "Any questions?" "Did you all get that?" "Everybody understand?" or "Does that make sense?"

Rather than respond to these questions, most learners will sit quietly, and the lecturer doesn't know whether they understand, they are too confused to answer, they think they get it (but are off base), or they are too embarrassed to show their lack of understanding in front of others. Such general questions are simply not sufficient in determining whether or not students "get it."

Additionally, students aren't always self-regulated learners. They may not be aware of what they do or do not understand. They sometimes think they get it, when they really don't (Hofer, Yu, & Pintrich, 1998). If you doubt this, consider how often you have heard students comment, "I thought I knew this stuff, but I bombed the exam."

Most of the checking for understanding done in schools is ineffective. Thankfully, there are a number of ways to address the situation. We've organized this book, and the ways that teachers can check for understanding, into larger categories, including oral language, questioning, writing, projects and performances, tests, and schoolwide approaches. In this chapter, we'll explore checking for understanding in terms of what it is, what it is not, and how it links to other teaching initiatives.

What Is Checking for Understanding?

Checking for understanding is an important step in the teaching and learning process. The background knowledge that students bring into the classroom influences how they understand the material you share and the lessons or learning opportunities you provide. Unless you check for understanding, it is difficult to know exactly what students are getting out of the lesson.

Research suggests that an important part of the learning process in all content areas is identifying and confronting misconceptions that can interfere with learning. Consider, for instance, how appreciating and addressing students' misconceptions can inform instruction in the following areas:

- Incorrect beliefs of young children that paintings are produced in factories (Wolf, 1987)
- Elementary students' misunderstanding that an equal sign in mathematics indicates an operation, rather than a relation (Ginsburg, 1982)
- K–3 students' beliefs that Native Americans who lived in tepees did so because they were poor and could not afford a house (Brophy & Alleman, 2002)
- Mistaken beliefs about living creatures, for example, that flies can walk on the ceiling because they have suction cups on their feet, and beavers use their tails as a trowel (Smith, 1920)
- Science students' misconception that larger objects are heavier than smaller ones (Schauble, 1996)
- The belief by adolescents (and adults) that there is a greater likelihood of "tails" in a coin toss after a series of "heads"—also known as the "Gambler's Fallacy" (Shaughnessy, 1977)

The act of checking for understanding not only corrects misconceptions; it can also improve learning. In a study by Vosniadou, Ioannides, Dimitrakopoulou, and Papademetriou (2001), two groups of students participated in a physics lesson.

With one group of students, the researchers checked for understanding before moving on to the next part of the lesson. They did so by presenting students with a brief scenario and asking them to predict and explain the outcome. The other group participated in the exact same lesson but without any pauses to check for understanding. As you might expect, the findings clearly demonstrated that the first group had a significantly greater increase in post-test over pre-test performance on assessments of content knowledge.

In addition, checking for understanding provides students with a model of good study skills. When their teachers regularly check for understanding, students become increasingly aware of how to monitor their own understanding. In the classic study by Bloom and Broder (1950), students performing well below grade level were paired with students who were successful. The successful students shared the variety of ways that they used to check that they understood the material. For example, the successful students restated sections of the material in their own words, asked themselves questions about the material, and thought of examples that related to the information they were reading. The students identified as at risk of school failure first observed and then began to incorporate these strategies into their own studying. Results of this study showed a significant improvement in comprehension test scores for the students who had been performing below grade level. These findings held when the performance changes were compared with a control group who spent the same amount of time with the material but did not receive any guidance in checking their own understanding from peers.

What Checking for Understanding Is Not

Checking for understanding is not the final exam or the state achievement tests. While there is evidence that checking for understanding will improve the scores students receive on these types of assessments, they are not what we mean by checking for understanding. Final exams and state standards tests are summative exams. They are designed to provide feedback on how the student performed after instruction.

Checking for understanding is a systematic approach to formative assessment. Let's explore the difference between formative and summative assessment in greater detail. Figure 1.1 provides a comparison between the two assessment systems.

Figure 1.1	Comparison of Formative and Summative Assessments	
	Formative Assessments	**Summative Assessments**
Purpose	To improve instruction and provide student feedback	To measure student competency
When administered	Ongoing throughout unit	End of unit or course
How students use results	To self-monitor understanding	To gauge their progress toward course or grade-level goals and benchmarks
How teachers use results	To check for understanding	For grades, promotion

Formative assessments are ongoing assessments, reviews, and observations in a classroom. Teachers use formative assessment to improve instructional methods and provide student feedback throughout the teaching and learning process. For example, if a teacher observes that some students do not grasp a concept, he or she can design a review activity to reinforce the concept or use a different instructional strategy to reteach it. (At the very least, teachers should check for understanding every 15 minutes; we have colleagues who check for understanding every couple of minutes.) Likewise, students can monitor their progress by looking at their results on periodic quizzes and performance tasks. The results of formative assessments are used to modify and validate instruction.

Summative assessments are typically used to evaluate the effectiveness of instructional programs and services at the end of an academic year or at a pre-determined time. The goal of summative assessments is to judge student competency after an instructional phase is complete. For example, the Florida Comprehensive Assessment Test administered to students in Florida once a year is a summative assessment of each student's ability at certain points in time. Summative evaluations are used to determine if students have mastered specific competencies and to identify instructional areas that need additional attention. The cartoon in Figure 1.2 futher illustrates the difference between formative and summative assessments.

Figure 1.2	True Learning?

It is assessment which
helps us distinguish between
teaching and learning.

© King Features Syndicate.

How Is Checking for Understanding Related to Other Teaching Initiatives?

There is no shortage of ideas for improving schools. An adaptation of a common saying hangs on our office wall that reads: "So many initiatives, so little time." This message reminds us on a daily basis that there is limited time to make progress; we have to pick and choose our initiatives wisely. Similarly, when our selected initiatives are conceptually linked, we know that we are more likely to implement them and see their widespread use. Let's consider how checking for understanding is related to some of the more common initiatives in education.

Understanding by Design

In 1998, Wiggins and McTighe proposed a curriculum model called Understanding by Design, in which curriculum and instruction are developed "backward." Teachers and curriculum developers learned to begin with the end in mind and plan accordingly. In other words, Wiggins and McTighe implored us to think about the outcomes, goals, and objectives we had for student learning first and then plan instruction and develop curriculum to close the gap between what students already know and what they need to know. A graphic representation of the stages in the backward curriculum design process can be found in Figure 1.3.

Figure 1.3	Stages in the Backward Design Process

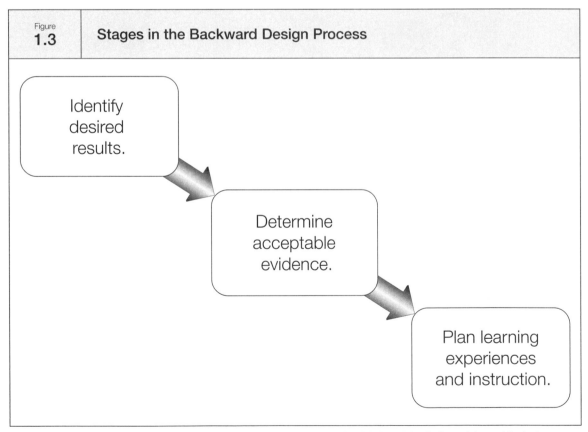

From *Understanding by design* (p. 9), by G. Wiggins and J. McTighe, 1998, Alexandria, VA: Association for Supervision and Curriculum Development.

A significant part of the Understanding by Design model centers on the use of assessments that focus on student understanding. As Wiggins and McTighe note, "Because understanding develops as a result of ongoing inquiry and rethinking, the assessment of understanding should be thought of in terms of a collection of evidence over time instead of an event—a single moment-in-time test at the end of instruction." (1988, p. 13)

Wiggins and McTighe offer an additional tool for thinking about how we check for understanding. They describe a nested framework that focuses on prioritizing curricular priorities in order to teach essential knowledge (see Figure 1.4). The innermost circle represents the area on which we want to spend more of our time—the enduring understanding. The second concentric circle represents things that are important to know and be able to do. The outermost circle encompasses information that is worth being familiar with.

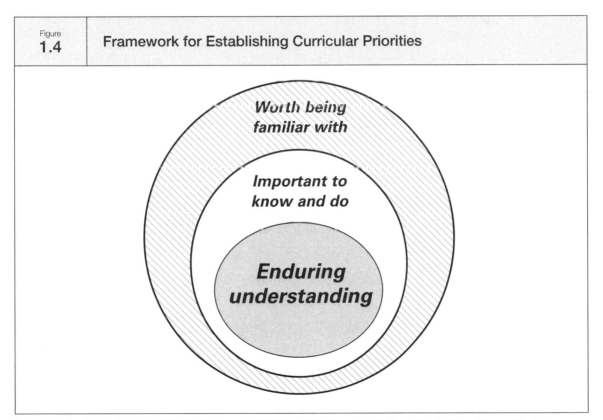

| Figure 1.4 | Framework for Establishing Curricular Priorities |

Worth being familiar with

Important to know and do

Enduring understanding

From *Understanding by design* (p. 10), by G. Wiggins and J. McTighe, 1998, Alexandria, VA: Association for Supervision and Curriculum Development.

Note that the enduring understanding is embedded in the other two; content from the outer circles is needed to arrive at those "big ideas." However, the authors ask us as educators to weigh the relative importance of what we teach. For example, if our lessons focus heavily on things worth being familiar with but do not serve as a pathway to enduring understanding, we are likely squandering valuable instructional time. The framework serves as a way of prioritizing how we check for understanding and what we check.

Differentiating Instruction

Carol Ann Tomlinson (1999) has challenged educators to differentiate instruction to meet the increasingly diverse needs of students. As noted in Figure 1.5, there are a number of ways to accomplish this task. Teachers can differentiate the content, process, or products they use or expect from students.

As noted in Tomlinson's model, assessment serves a critical role in teacher decision making. Teachers need to use a wide variety of assessment systems (and regularly check our students' understanding) to know whether or not our instructional interventions, modifications, accommodations, and extensions are working.

Checking for understanding presumes that students are able to demonstrate their understanding in different ways. This demands not only that products are differentiated but also that our ways of analyzing them are differentiated. Consider this example of a student's different responses to the same question.

Mariana, a 5th grader, was uncomfortable with her command of English and reluctant to speak in class. Mariana's teacher, Aida Allen, asked her to describe the character of Byron, the oldest brother in *The Watsons Go to Birmingham—1963* (Curtis, 1995). Byron is the kind of big brother who torments his younger siblings, sometimes making their lives miserable. However, his love for his brother and sister manifests itself in some surprising ways. Readers usually respond to Byron strongly, as his hurtful acts and flashes of kindness elevate him to the level of a realistic character. But in reply to Ms. Allen, Mariana merely mumbled, "Mean." Ms. Allen knew that Mariana had been enjoying the book and had overheard her talking to another member of her book club about it. A teacher who didn't understand checking for understanding might have cajoled Mariana for a minute or two and then moved on to another student who would supply a richer answer. But because she was interested in checking Mariana's understanding and not just filling the room with one

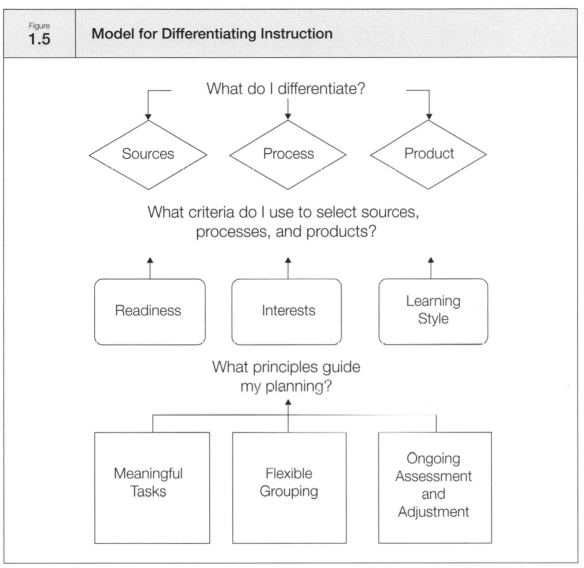

| Figure 1.5 | **Model for Differentiating Instruction** |

Adapted from *The differentiated classroom: Responding to the needs of all learners* (p. 17), by C. A. Tomlinson, 1999, Alexandria, VA: Association for Supervision and Curriculum Development.

student's answer, Ms. Allen later gave Mariana and a few other students character maps. "I'd like to know what you think about the main characters in this book and what evidence you have to support your opinions," she said. Mariana, uncomfortable with talking in class but engaged with the book, completed a character map of Byron in less than 10 minutes (see Figure 1.6). Her written response offered a

Figure 1.6	Mariana's Character Map

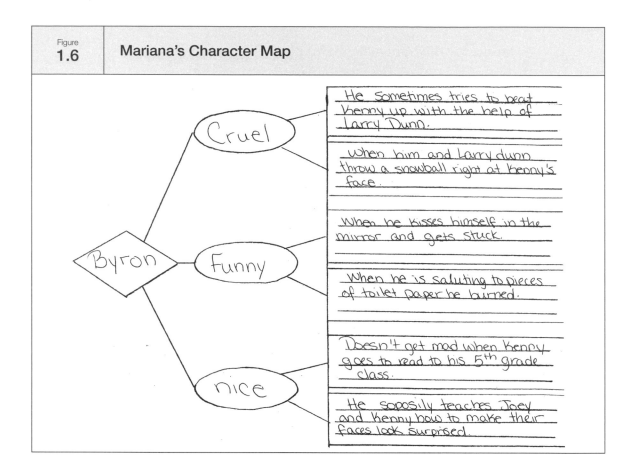

far richer snapshot of her understanding than the monosyllabic answer she had supplied earlier. Because she was persistent in differentiating product to check for understanding, Ms. Allen could see that Mariana understood far more than she had originally demonstrated.

Closing the Achievement Gap

Despite decades of attention, achievement gaps persist. When comparing student achievement data at aggregate levels, differences based on ethnicity and race, language, and gender are obvious. The North Central Regional Educational Laboratory assembled a group of researchers, policymakers, and practitioners who summarized what is currently known about the achievement gap. Their analysis suggests that the achievement gap has three dimensions: (1) factors contributing to the gap, such as poverty, race, and teacher quality; (2) multiple contexts in which the achievement gap exists, such as in-school and out-of-school factors; and (3) time, as students progress through their education from preK to grade 12 and beyond (Bennett et al., 2004).

Obviously, some of these factors are more easily addressed by teachers and administrators than others. While we know that poverty, for example, plays a significant role in the achievement gap, a teacher is unlikely to effect change in that area. What is more easily addressed is the time that students have in school and the quality of the teachers they interact with. Teachers have no time to waste. We need to focus our instruction and ensure that students are learning, thinking, understanding, comprehending, and processing at high levels. We can only do this when we regularly check for understanding.

Breakthrough

The final theoretical framework we'll discuss is the work of Fullan, Hill, and Crévola (2006) and their Breakthrough model of school reform. They call for a shift in school culture that uses data to make decisions in order to personalize instruction. They are not calling for prescriptive teaching, which they acknowledge can "lead to short-term gains, but [at] a price paid in terms of narrow control for teachers and little control for students" (p. 11). Instead, they advocate for precision teaching that is data driven and provides feedback to students to monitor their own learning. Borrowing from a health care model called critical path analysis, the authors posit that students can benefit from educational systems that anticipate learning pathways and potential areas of difficulty. A critical path approach requires teachers to know the curriculum deeply (an expert model) and to be knowledgeable of the ways in which learner progress can be checked along the way (checking for understanding).

They say that a picture is worth a thousand words; for us a picture came to us serendipitously. In 2006, we attended the American Education Research Association conference. We arrived early to the room where we were scheduled to present. As it happened, Dr. Jianyu Wang (2006), a professor of physical education and kinesiology from California State University, Bakersfield, was just finishing his presentation of his research on understanding the developmental needs of badminton players by analyzing their performance. He shared a conceptual map of assessment (see Figure 1.7).

We were astounded. Dr. Wang's research was evidence of what we have been talking about. Close observation, deep knowledge of developmental processes, and content expertise had yielded a critical path analysis that anticipated the permutations a learner might take in learning badminton.

We are not suggesting that all learning needs to be formatted into a conceptual map like Wang's (although it is certainly impressive). But it gave us pause about the ways in which curriculum and student performance are understood. A physical education teacher using this conceptual approach would not wait until the final score of a match to determine whether the athlete understood badminton. The teacher would assess the player's performance based on skills like arm and trunk action. The teacher would note not only whether strokes were effective or ineffective but also what made them so. Yet how often are checks for understanding implemented too late, at the end of a unit? How often does only the number of correct responses define those checks? Checking for understanding should do the following:

- Align with enduring understandings (Wiggins & McTighe, 1998)
- Allow for differentiation (Tomlinson, 1999)
- Focus on gap analysis (Bennett et al., 2004)
- Lead to precise teaching (Fullan et al., 2006)

In other words, checking for understanding should become part of the routine of teaching. Unfortunately, as Schmoker (2006) notes, "an enormous proportion of daily assessments are simply never assessed—formally or informally. For the majority of lessons, no evidence exists by which a teacher could gauge or report on how well students are learning essential standards" (p. 16).

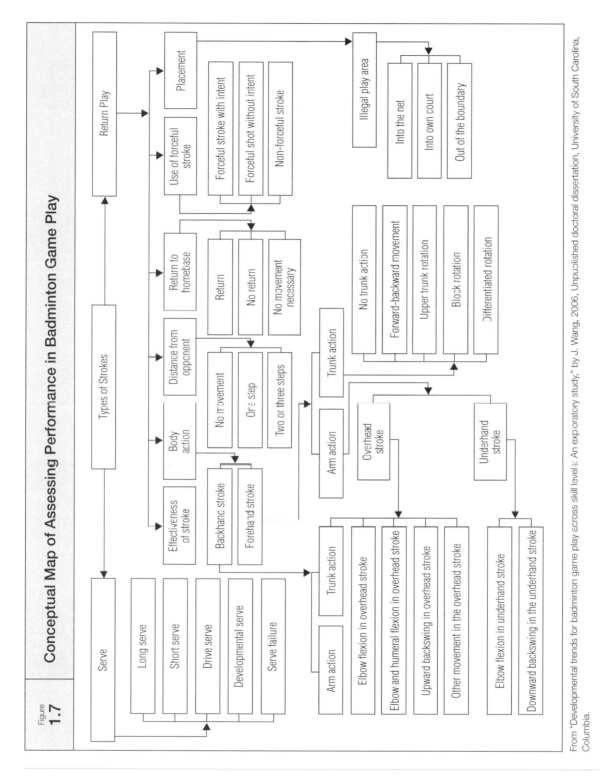

Figure 1.7 Conceptual Map of Assessing Performance in Badminton Game Play

From "Developmental trends for badminton game play across skill levels: An exploratory study," by J. Wang, 2006, Unpublished doctoral dissertation, University of South Carolina, Columbia.

Conclusion

Checking for understanding completes the circle of assessment, planning, and instruction by providing teachers and students with evidence of learning. In addition, it is consistent with several other educational innovations, including Understanding by Design and differentiated instruction. Use these guiding questions to incorporate checking for understanding in your practice:

- Do I know what misconceptions or naïve assumptions my students possess?
- How do I know what they understand?
- What evidence will I accept for this understanding?
- How will I use their understandings to plan future instruction?

2

Using Oral Language to Check for Understanding

Humans have been using their voices to engage in critical and creative thinking for a long time—much longer, in fact, than they have used writing instruments. Sumerian cuneiforms, the first writing system, were not developed until about 4000 BCE (Ouaknin, 1999). This is a relatively short amount of time when you consider that humans have been communicating orally for at least 50,000 years (Ong, 1991). Interestingly, there are thousands of languages that have no written literature associated with them. As Ong (1991) notes:

> Indeed, language is so overwhelmingly oral that of all the many thousands of languages—possibly tens of thousands—spoken in the course of human history only around 106 have ever been committed to a degree sufficient to have produced literature, and most have never been written at all. Of the some 3,000 languages spoken that exist today only some 78 have a literature. (p. 7)

That isn't to say that oral traditions are inadequate. Humans have a long history of using oral language to communicate with one another. Oral language has served us well in conveying information that keeps members of our communities alive, healthy, safe, and fed.

The classroom is no exception to these oral traditions. In a book focused on the ways in which teachers and students interact, it seems appropriate to begin with the oldest language tradition—oral. We'll define oral language first, explore the development of oral language, review some cautionary evidence of the misuse of oral language in the classroom, and then explore the ways in which oral language can be used in checking for understanding.

Oral Language Defined

We've adopted the speaking and listening definitions put forth by Cooper and Morreale:

> **Speaking:** Speaking is the uniquely human act or process of sharing and exchanging information, ideas, and emotions using oral language. Whether in daily information interactions or in more formal settings, communicators are required to organize coherent messages, deliver them clearly, and adapt them to their listeners.
>
> **Listening:** Listening is the process of receiving, constructing meaning from, and responding to spoken and/or nonverbal messages. People call on different listening skills depending on whether their goal is to comprehend information, critique and evaluate a message, show empathy for the feelings expressed by others, or appreciate a performance. Taken together, the communication skills of speaking and listening, called *oral language*, form the basis for thinking. (2003, p. x)

In addition to these general definitions of speaking and listening, there are other language registers that humans use to communicate. In her work on understanding poverty, Payne (1995) delineates five distinct language registers. Each of these is explained in Figure 2.1. Speakers need to recognize these language registers, use them appropriately for the setting, and move fluidly between registers. As Romaine (1994) notes, "The concept of register is typically concerned with variations in language conditioned by uses rather than users and involves consideration of the situation or context of use, the purpose, subject-matter, and content of the message, and the relationship between the participants" (p. 20).

Figure 2.1	Language Registers

Fixed or frozen. Fixed speech is reserved for traditions in which the language does not change. Examples of fixed speech include the Pledge of Allegiance, Shakespeare plays, and civil ceremonies such as weddings.

Formal. At the formal level, speech is expected to be presented in complete sentences with specific word usage. Formal language is the standard for work, school, and business and is more often seen in writing than in speaking. However, public speeches and presentations are expected to be delivered in a formal language register.

Consultative. The third level of language, consultative, is a formal register used in conversations. Less appropriate for writing, students often use consultative language in their interactions in the classroom.

Casual. This is the language that is used in conversation with friends. In casual speech, word choice is general and conversation is dependent upon nonverbal assists, significant background knowledge, and shared information.

Intimate. This is the language used by very close friends and lovers. Intimate speech is private and often requires a significant amount of shared history, knowledge, and experience.

From *Language arts workshop: Purposeful reading and writing instruction* (p. 210), by N. Frey and D. Fisher, 2006, Upper Saddle River, NJ: Pearson/Merrill/Prentice Hall.

Oral Language Development

Oral language development is not simply teaching children to speak. Oral language development must focus on students' ability to communicate more effectively. Oral language involves thinking, knowledge, and skills that develop across the life span. These are critical because "speaking and listening are to reading and writing [as] walking is to running" (New Standards, 2001, p. i).

Oral language development is a natural process for children and youth. It occurs almost without effort. While the ability to communicate improves as students get older, such growth will not automatically lead to high levels of performance and skill. To speak in highly effective ways requires attention and practice. Unfortunately, as Stabb (1986) notes, teachers often become "so involved with establishing routine, finishing the textbook, covering curriculum, and preparing students for standardized tests that we have forgotten one of our original goals, that of stimulating thought" (p. 290).

A great deal is known about the oral language development of young children (see Biemiller, 1999; Kirkland & Patterson, 2005). As noted in Figure 2.2, researchers, parents, and teachers have articulated developmental milestones for children's acquisition of oral communication skills. Much less is known about oral language development for older students. However, some school districts, such as Long Beach Unified School District in California, have established goals for oral language across the grade levels (see Figure 2.3).

Figure 2.2	Stages of Early Oral Language Development	
STAGE	AGE	DESCRIPTION
Stage 1	Infant	A child at this stage smiles socially, imitates facial expressions, coos, cries, babbles, plays with sounds, develops intonation, and repeats syllables.
Stage 2	18 months to 2 years	A child at this stage responds to specific songs, uses two-word sentences, depends on intonation and gesture, understands simple questions, and points to and/or names objects in pictures.
Stage 3	2 to 3 years	A child at this stage begins to use pronouns and prepositions, uses "no," remembers names of objects, and generalizes. There is a high interest in language and an increase in communication. There is a large jump in vocabulary growth and articulation.
Stage 4	3 to 4 years	A child at this stage communicates needs, asks questions, begins to enjoy humor, has much better articulation, begins true conversation, responds to directional commands, knows parts of songs, can retell a story, speaks in three- and four-word sentences, is acquiring the rules of grammar, and learns sophisticated words heard in adult conversation.
Stage 5	4 to 5 years	A child at this stage has a tremendous vocabulary, uses irregular noun and verb forms, talks with adults on adult level in four- to eight-word sentences, giggles over nonsense words, engages in imaginative play using complex oral scripts, tells longer stories, recounts in sequence the day's events, and uses silly and profane language to experiment and shock the listener.

Adapted from *The portfolio and its use: A road map for assessment,* by S. MacDonald, 1997, Little Rock, AR: Southern Early Childhood Association.

There is a significant body of evidence on the importance of attending to oral language development for English language learners across the K–12 spectrum (Rothenberg & Fisher, 2007; Short & Echevarria, 2004/2005). Given that oral language is the foundation of print literacy, it seems reasonable to suggest that all teachers, and especially those who teach English language learners, focus on speaking and listening in the classroom.

Figure 2.3	Goals for Speaking and Listening by Grade Levels

Kindergarten–2nd Grade

Students listen critically and respond appropriately to oral communication. Students will:

- Determine the purpose or purposes of listening (e.g., to obtain information, to solve problems, for enjoyment)
- Ask for clarification and explanation of stories and ideas
- Paraphrase information that has been shared orally by others
- Give and follow three- and four-step oral directions
- Speak clearly and at an appropriate pace for the type of communication (e.g., informal discussion, report to class)

Students deliver brief recitations and oral presentations about familiar experiences or interests. Students will:

- Describe story elements (e.g., characters, plot, setting)
- Report on a topic with facts and details, drawing from several sources of information

3rd–5th Grade

Students deliver focused, coherent presentations that convey ideas clearly and relate to the background and interests of the audience. Students will:

- Ask questions that seek information not already discussed
- Interpret a speaker's verbal and nonverbal messages, purposes, and perspectives
- Make inferences or draw conclusions based on an oral report
- Retell, paraphrase, and explain what has been said by the speaker typically listened to for recreational, informational, or functional purposes
- Select a focus, organizational structure, and point of view for an oral presentation
- Clarify and support spoken ideas with evidence and examples
- Analyze media sources for information, entertainment, persuasion, interpretation of events, and transmission of culture

Students deliver well-organized formal presentations employing traditional rhetorical strategies (e.g., narration, exposition, persuasion, description). Students will:

- Deliver narrative presentations that establish a situation, plot, point of view, and setting with descriptive words and phrases and show, rather than tell, the listener what happens
- Deliver informative presentations about an important idea, issue, or event by framing questions to direct the investigation, establishing a controlling idea or topic, and developing the topic with simple facts, details, examples, and explanations
- Deliver oral responses to literature that summarize significant events and details, articulate an understanding of several ideas or images communicated by the literary work, and use examples or textual evidence from the work to support conclusions

Figure 2.3	Goals for Speaking and Listening by Grade Levels (*continued*)

6th–8th Grade

Students formulate adroit judgments about oral communication. They deliver focused and coherent presentations that convey clear and distinct perspectives and demonstrate solid reasoning. They use gestures, tone, and vocabulary tailored to the audience and purpose. Students will:

- Paraphrase a speaker's purpose and point of view and ask relevant questions concerning the speaker's content, delivery, and purpose

- Deliver a focused, coherent speech based on organized information that generally includes an introduction, transitions, preview and summaries, a logical body, and an effective conclusion

- Evaluate the credibility of a speaker and evaluate the various ways in which visual image makers communicate information and affect impressions and opinions

- Demonstrate appropriate group discussion behavior by listening attentively, collaborating equitably, and asking questions and extending discussions

Students deliver polished formal and extemporaneous presentations that combine traditional rhetorical strategies of narration, exposition, persuasion, and description. Student speaking demonstrates a command of standard American English and the organizational and delivery strategies outlined in the California ELA Standards. Students will:

- Deliver narrative presentations that relate a coherent incident, event, or situation and elegantly express the significance of, and the subject's attitude about, the incident, event, or situation

- Deliver oral responses to literature that interpret the reading and provide insight through textual references, with judgments supported and discussed using text connections (text-to-self, text-to-text, and text-to-world)

- Deliver research presentations that define a thesis, express important ideas using direct quotations from significant sources, and utilize visuals (charts, maps, and graphs) as a tool for presenting important information

- Deliver persuasive presentations that use supportive arguments with detailed evidence, examples, and reasoning and that anticipate and answer listener concerns and counterarguments effectively

- Recite poems, sections of speeches, or dramatic soliloquies using voice modulation, tone, and gestures expressively to enhance the meaning

From "Goals for speaking and listening by grade levels," from the Office of Curriculum, Instruction, and Professional Development, Long Beach Unified School District.

Misuses of Oral Language in the Classroom

Regardless of the size of the school, its demographics, the age of the teaching staff, or any other factor that we can think of, oral language will be used in the classroom. People will talk and listen—that's a given. The ways in which this talking and listening are used are the real key. There are at least three areas that we should address before continuing our discussion of the use of oral language in checking for understanding: poverty, language, and perceived skill level; gender differences; and the Initiate-Respond-Evaluate model of questioning.

Poverty, Language, and Perceived Skill Level

In classrooms where there are increased numbers of students living in poverty, teachers talk more and students talk less (Lingard, Hayes, & Mills, 2003). In addition, there is an increased focus on basic skills in these classrooms and less attention to critical and creative thinking (Stipek, 2004). Teachers of struggling student groups or tracks usually offer students "less exciting instruction, less emphasis on meaning and conceptualization, and more rote drill and practice activities" than do teachers of high-performing or heterogeneous groups and classes (Cotton, 1989).

English language learners in many classrooms are asked easier questions or no questions at all (Guan Eng Ho, 2005; Rothenberg & Fisher, 2007). Several decades ago, Flanders (1970) noted that teachers of high-achieving students talked 55 percent of the class time. He compared them with teachers of low-achieving students who monopolized class time, talking at least 80 percent of the time.

In other words, the amount of teacher versus student talk in a classroom varies by the demographics of the students. In addition, students who live in poverty, are English language learners, have disabilities, or are otherwise at risk in school spend more of their time on basic skills and less time engaged in activities, lessons, or inquiry that fosters creative and critical thinking.

Gender Differences

Interestingly, gender also plays a role in how much talk there is in a classroom. While there are debates on which gender is at greater risk for school failure and lack of engagement (van Langen, Bosker, & Dekkers, 2006; Wilhelm & Smith, 2005), there is clear evidence that the amount of time that girls spend participating orally in class decreases as they get older (Orenstein, 1994). In addition, there is evidence that teachers call on boys more often than girls, ask boys more higher-order questions, give boys more extensive feedback, and use longer wait time with boys than with girls (Sadker & Sadker, 1986, 1995).

The Initiate-Respond-Evaluate Model

In classrooms across the country, teachers ask students questions and students respond. The Initiate-Respond-Evaluate model of questioning dominates classroom discourse (see Cazden, 1988). In this model, the teacher asks a question, specific students are called on to answer the question, and the teacher evaluates the response. A typical interaction might look something like this:

Teacher: Why did the Puritans leave England? (*Initiate*)
Student: Because they were not treated right because of their religion. (*Respond*)
Teacher: Yes. (*Evaluate*) And why else? (*Initiate*)

While this interaction requires oral language, it focuses on "guess what's in the teacher's head" or what the teacher already knows, not on critical thinking by the whole group. In addition, when one student is provided the opportunity to answer, the ability to check for understanding with the larger group is lost. Cazden (1988) suggests that teachers ask themselves two questions about the discourse in their classrooms:

- How do patterns of talk in the classroom affect the quality of students' educational opportunities and outcomes?
- How is discourse used as a support for deeper student learning?

Let's explore these questions as we consider the ways in which teachers can proactively and positively use oral language to check for understanding.

Oral Language Strategies in Checking for Understanding

Accountable Talk

How often have you assigned a partner discussion topic to students, only to hear the conversation devolve into a chat about weekend activities, a new movie, or the lunch menu? Often these students are not being willfully disobedient, but rather lack the skills necessary to conduct a meaningful conversation about an academic topic. Accountable talk is a framework for teaching students about discourse in order to enrich these interactions. First developed by Lauren Resnick (2000) and a team of researchers at the Institute for Learning at the University of Pittsburgh, accountable talk describes the agreements students and their teacher commit to as they engage in partner conversations. These include the following guidelines:

- Stay on topic.
- Use information that is accurate and appropriate for the topic.
- Think deeply about what the partner has to say.

We consider accountable talk to be crucial to classroom discourse because it creates shared expectations for all academic communication in the classroom. The three principles are equally relevant in a guided reading group, a book club meeting, a Socratic seminar, or a whole-class discussion.

Students are taught how to be accountable to one another and to their learning using techniques that forward the conversation and deepen their understanding of the topic at hand. The Institute for Learning Web site (www.instituteforlearning. org) describes five indicators of accountable talk; we have added an example after each:

- Press for clarification and explanation: "Could you describe what you mean?"
- Require justification of proposals and challenges: "Where did you find that information?"
- Recognize and challenge misconceptions: "I don't agree because . . ."
- Demand evidence for claims and arguments: "Can you give me an example?"
- Interpret and use each other's statements: "David suggested . . ."

These communication skills are invaluable for students using inquiry as a way to engage in active learning. Teachers fostering accountable talk in the classroom can monitor the use of these indicators by listening to partners exchange information. In addition, the questions students ask of one another should inform the next segment of teacher-directed instruction.

Sixth grade teacher Ricardo Montoya monitors partner conversations to make teaching decisions. During one lesson, he introduced the concept of physical and chemical weathering to students, assigned them to partner groups, and asked the partners to identify examples of the two types of weathering using a series of photographs. As Mr. Montoya listened in on the students' conversations, he noticed that several partners were asking clarifying questions of one another concerning a photograph of acid rain. A few partners felt it was an example of physical weathering because of the force of the water. Many others described it as chemical weathering due to the acidic quality of the rain. Mr. Montoya asked partners to share their conversations, including their disagreements, with the rest of the class. He then led a class discussion on the possibility of considering acid rain as an example of both chemical and physical weathering. Mr. Montoya's attention to the students' conversations helped him to make the next instructional step in his lesson.

Noticing Nonverbal Cues

Another way that teachers use oral language to check for understanding involves noticing the nonverbal cues that students give. While it may seem a stretch to include nonverbal cues in typical oral language interactions, remember that a significant portion of our communication comes from facial expression, eye movement, and such (see Calero, 2005). Students in our classrooms often let us know that they do or do not understand something through nonverbal cues, which may be as simple as the look on one's face or as complex as throwing one's hands in the air (in triumph over a math problem or in agony over a reading assignment). As a teacher, you can use nonverbal cues to determine if your students look puzzled, harried, or bored. With practice, you will find yourself noticing and responding to these nonverbal cues while teaching.

Fifth grade teacher Amanda Chavez uses a daily shared reading lesson to model her thinking and comprehension strategies for students. She knows that her modeling will provide students with increasingly complex ways of thinking about texts. During her shared reading about Sojourner Truth from *Americans Who Tell the Truth* (Shetterly, 2005), Ms. Chavez noticed that Angel had a puzzled look on her face. Ms. Chavez paused in her reading and added some background information, watching Angel's face the whole time for signs of understanding. When Ms. Chavez said, "It seems strange now, but during the times of slavery, people could sell children who were born into slavery," Angel's face changed noticeably. It became clear that Angel couldn't grasp the text about Sojourner Truth's life until she had the understanding that people have sold children.

Value Lineups

Many students master the skill of explaining their own position on a topic, but fewer learn the art of listening to positions that differ from their own. However, this ability is at the heart of meaningful discourse in the classroom and is essential to all learning. In a truly learner-centered classroom, there is a free exchange of ideas that results in arriving at solutions to problems. Active learning results not from a knowledge dump emanating from the teacher alone but from a deeper understanding of the nuances and shades of gray that elevate knowledge. The National Research Council (2000) contrasts experts with novices in this way:

> Experts first seek to develop an understanding of problems, and this often involves thinking in terms of core concepts or big ideas. . . . Novices' knowledge is much less likely to be organized around big ideas; they are more likely to approach problems by searching for correct formulas and pat answers that fit their everyday intuitions. (p. 49)

Value lineups help students to develop such in-depth knowledge by enabling them to explore core concepts and understand problems by having them first analyze their beliefs and then listen to the positions held by others. The value lineup is a structure for fostering peer discourse based on students' opinions about an academic topic (Kagan, 1994). Students are asked to evaluate a statement and instructed to line up according to their degree of agreement or disagreement with the statement. After forming a single line, the queue is then folded in half so that the students who most strongly agreed and disagreed with one another are now face to face. Students then discuss their reasons for their positions and listen to the perspectives of their partners. This cultivates a broader understanding of the distinctions of understanding on a topic.

When Deborah Chin's 10th grade biology students were beginning a unit on the use of cloning, she asked them to consider their values and beliefs about cloning in reaction to this statement: "Scientists should be allowed to pursue research in cloning." Ms. Chin's class then placed themselves on the wall of the classroom where the numbers 1 through 5 were displayed in a Likert-type scale. She reminded them that a 5 meant they strongly agreed, 4 meant they agreed, 3 meant they were not sure, 2 meant they disagreed, and 1 indicated that they strongly disagreed.

The students spent the next two minutes lining up according to their opinions. Ms. Chin then located the 18th student in line (the halfway point in this class of 36) and folded the line in half. Now the first student spoke to the 36th student, the second spoke to the 35th, and so on. Ms. Chin walked the line, listening to their conversations about why they agreed or disagreed with scientific research on cloning. She heard Anne, who strongly agreed, explaining to Paul, who strongly disagreed, about her recent trip with her family to Yosemite: "There's this project to clone the champion trees of the country so that they can be planted in other places, especially in cities." She went on to explain that champion trees are the largest of their species and possess unique genetic features that make them more durable. Paul remarked that he never thought of cloning trees, only of humans, even though Ms. Chin's question did not mention this.

After several minutes of conversation, Ms. Chin instructed students to return to their seats. The lively debate continued, but important information from multiple perspectives was shared in the discussion. A number of factors were introduced to the problem of cloning, including benefits and moral and religious objections. By using the value lineup, Ms. Chin was able to assess preconceived notions, background knowledge, and gaps in information. In addition, her students were challenged to consider other perspectives on the topic.

Retellings

Retellings are new accounts or adaptations of a text that allow students to consider information and then summarize, orally, what they understand about this information. Retellings require that students processing large segments of text think about the sequence of ideas or events and their importance. Inviting students to retell what they have just heard or read is a powerful way of checking for under-standing (Hansen, 2004; Shaw, 2005).

Gambrell, Koskinen, and Kapinus (1991) examined the use of retellings with 4th grade proficient and less-proficient readers. They found that students who employed this technique made significant increases in the number of propositions and story structure elements recalled as well as the overall number of comprehension questions answered correctly. These authors note that students needed at least four practice sessions with retelling to become comfortable with the strategy. Like Cambourne (1998), Gambrell and colleagues argue that retelling is a more effective postreading activity than teacher questioning.

As noted above, students need to be taught the procedures of retelling. Under-standing these processes helps establish purpose in reading and guides students' attention to key information from the text that they can use in their retellings. Figure 2.4 provides a number of variations on retellings, some of which, also known as summaries, will be discussed in the next chapter on using writing to check for understanding. In introducing the retelling technique, teachers should do the following:

1. Explain that the purpose of a retelling is to re-create the text in your own words.
2. Ask students to discuss the ways in which they talk about their favorite movie or CD. Make the connection between talking about the movie or CD and talking about a piece of text.
3. Model a retelling from a short piece of familiar text for students. If students know the piece of text well, they can compare the original with the retelling.
4. After the modeled retelling, ask students to discuss the similarities and differences between the original and the retelling.
5. Select a new piece of text, read it aloud, and create a retelling as a group. Again, ask students to discuss the similarities and differences between the original and the retelling.

As students become increasingly familiar with retellings, they can be used to check for understanding.

Figure 2.4	**Variations on Retellings**
Oral to Oral Oral to Written Oral to Video	Listens to a selection and retells it orally Listens to a selection and retells it in writing (summary) Listens to a selection and creates a video or movie of it
Reading to Oral Reading to Written Reading to Video	Reads a selection and retells it orally Reads a selection and retells it in writing (summary) Reads a selection and creates a video or movie of it
Viewing to Oral Viewing to Written Viewing to Video	Views a film and retells it orally Views a film and retells it in writing (summary) Views a film and creates a video or movie of it

Fourth grade teacher Aida Allen used the story retelling rubric found in Figure 2.5 to check her students' understanding of fiction and story grammar. She introduced the rubric after reading aloud *Walter, the Farting Dog* (Kotzwinkle & Murray, 2001). As a class, they created a retelling. Ms. Allen then facilitated the students in a discussion of the rubric, and they evaluated their group retelling using this tool. Next, Ms. Allen gave each group of four students different picture books. Their task was to read the book together and create a small-group retelling. The books she selected were all from the Walter series: *Walter the Farting Dog Goes on a Cruise* (Kotzwinkle, Murray, & Gundy, 2006), *Rough Weather Ahead for Walter the Farting Dog* (Kotzwinkle, Murray, & Gundy, 2005), *Walter the Farting Dog: Trouble at the Yard Sale* (Kotzwinkle & Murray, 2004), and *Walter the Farting Dog Farts Again* (Kotzwinkle & Murray, 2005).

As each group presented their retelling, another group (assigned by Ms. Allen) used the retelling rubric to provide feedback. Ms. Allen reminded her students after each retelling that "we are all learning how to use the story retelling rubric—let's all help each other get really good at this."

Following several practices with using the story retelling rubric in groups, students were asked to meet with Ms. Allen individually to discuss and retell information from the books they were reading in their literature circles. The focus was on dog stories and included *Shiloh* (Naylor, 1991), *Where the Red Fern Grows: The Story of Two Dogs and a Boy* (Rawls, 1961), and *My Dog Skip* (Morris, 1995). Ms. Allen used the information she gathered during student retellings of the books they were reading to plan individual interventions as well as some whole-class lessons.

Figure 2.5	Retelling Rubric for Fiction			
Element	Exceeds Standards (2)	Meets Standards (1)	Needs Improvement (0)	Score
Characters	Your retelling describes the characters so that others have a good idea of what they are like.	Your retelling names the characters but does not describe much about them.	Your retelling confuses the identity of the characters or does not name them. Think about who was in the story and how they acted.	
Setting	Your retelling helps others get a clear idea of when and where the story took place.	Your retelling provides some details about where and when the story took place.	Your retelling needs to describe when and where the story took place.	
Problem	Your retelling describes the problem, why this problem occurred, and how it might be solved.	Your retelling names the problem but not how it occurred or might be solved.	Your retelling needs to describe the problem, how the problem developed, and how it might be solved.	
Solution	Your retelling focuses on how the characters solved the problem.	Your retelling includes some of the important events that led to the solution and most are in the correct order.	Your retelling needs to focus on the major events and how these events led to the solution to the problem	
Delivery	Your retelling uses good rhythm, fluency, expression, and gestures. Your voice changes for different characters.	Your rhythm and expression are good most of the time and you use some gestures. Your voice changes for some of the characters.	Your retelling needs to include expression and gestures. Your voice should change for different characters.	

Ms. Allen noted that her students rarely used dialogue during their retellings to discuss characters and the problems they faced. In subsequent shared readings, she modeled several retellings using character dialogue to address this whole-class need. Similarly, she noted that one student, Miriam, had difficulty with sequence; she met with Miriam during reading conferences and helped her use a graphic organizer to record events in order.

U.S. history teacher Jamie Ryan used the informational text retelling rubric shown in Figure 2.6 in her class for discussions about the textbook and primary source documents that her students read. During the course of study on the 1906 San Francisco earthquake, students read a number of primary source documents, including the proclamation by the mayor dated April 18, 1906. A number of primary source documents can be found on the Gilder Lehrman Institute for American History Web site (www.gilderlehrman.org). One student correctly noted in his retelling that the mayor had authorized the police to kill any looters they found. He also pointed out that the mayor's proclamation gave the police "exceptional powers—they could legally kill any person for ANY crime." The rubric allowed Ms. Ryan an opportunity to check her students' understanding of the various texts they read and to determine areas of need for each student.

Think-Pair-Share

Think-Pair-Share is a cooperative discussion strategy that allows students to discuss their responses with a peer before sharing with the whole class. Developed by Lyman (1981) and colleagues, there are three stages of student action:

1. **Think.** The teacher engages students' thinking with a question, prompt, reading, visual, or observation. The students should take a few minutes (not seconds) just to *think* about the question.
2. **Pair.** Using designated partners, students *pair* up to discuss their respective responses. They compare their thoughts and identify the responses they think are the best, most intriguing, most convincing, or most unique.
3. **Share.** After students talk in pairs for a few moments, the teacher asks pairs to *share* their thinking with the rest of the class.

Naturally, there are opportunities to check for understanding throughout the Think-Pair-Share activity. The teacher can listen in as pairs discuss their responses and can note the ways in which pairs share their responses.

In her 2nd grade class, Yazmine Sanchez invited her students to think about a person who made a difference. This introduction to a major 2nd grade social studies theme served to activate her students' background knowledge and to help them make connections with the curriculum they were about to study. After a few moments of thinking time, Ms. Sanchez asked her students to turn to a partner and talk about the person they were thinking of. Ms. Sanchez listened in on several students' pair conversations, noting their personal connections to the topic. She then invited pairs to share with the whole class. But she wasn't done yet; she continued this process with several additional questions, including the following:

Figure 2.6	Retelling Rubric for Informational Text			
Element	Exceeds Standards (2)	Meets Standards (1)	Needs Improvement (0)	Score
Key Ideas	Your retelling identifies all of the key ideas from the text.	Your retelling identifies a number of key ideas from the text.	Your retelling needs to identify and describe the key ideas from the text.	
Details	Your retelling helps others understand the text by providing details for each key idea.	Your retelling provides some details for some of the key ideas.	Your retelling needs to link details with key ideas.	
Sequence	Your retelling identifies a clear sequence of information that helps the listener understand the information.	Your retelling provides information in a sequence, but the sequence is slightly confused or out of order.	Your retelling needs to have a sequence that helps the listener understand.	
Conclusion	Your retelling ends with a conclusion that is directly linked to the information you provided.	Your retelling includes a concluding statement.	Your retelling needs to focus on the major idea from the text and needs to summarize the information gathered.	
Delivery	You use good rhythm, fluency, expression, and gestures.	Your rhythm and expression are good most of the time and you use some gestures.	Your retelling needs to include expression and gestures.	

- What did this person do that makes you think he or she made a difference?
- Who else do you know who made a difference?
- What characteristics are shared by people who make a difference?

With each question, Ms. Sanchez asked her students to think first, engage in a partner conversation, and then share their ideas with the whole class. Along the way, Ms. Sanchez made notes about what her students already knew, what misconceptions they had, and how they used language to express their ideas. Her checking for understanding was used to collect information that she could use in her instruction throughout the unit.

Similarly, high school government teacher Angie Jenkins uses Think-Pair-Share to engage her students in current government issues each day. During a discussion about immigration policy in the United States, students noted the potential changes to the policy. The variation Ms. Jenkins uses with her high school seniors is that they have to share their partner's thinking, not their own ideas. She does this to ensure that her students are listening and thinking as their partner talks, rather than forming rebuttal arguments. In one of the discussions on the changes to the immigration policy, Malik said, "My partner is going to participate in the walk out because she thinks that it's important to send a message and cost the government money. By not being here at school that day, she'll cost people money." Another student indicated, "Arian is going to come to school because she says that her mom came here to make sure she got an education."

The Think-Pair-Share time provides Ms. Jenkins with an opportunity to determine whether her students understand the current events that affect their lives and to ascertain if students still have any misunderstandings about these events in terms of government policy. She is interested not in changing their views of current events but in making sure that they can think critically about the events that will shape their experiences as adults.

Misconception Analysis

Misconceptions include preconceived notions, nonscientific beliefs, naive theories, mixed conceptions, or conceptual misunderstandings. Most of us have them and are not happy when we're told we're wrong about something, especially if it's something in our basic belief system. Children and youth are no different; they have misconceptions that interfere with their understanding of content or information and often are not readily willing to be challenged in these beliefs. As such, misconception analysis is an important part of checking for understanding.

Misconception analysis provides students an opportunity to discuss, often in small groups, misunderstandings that they have. Typically the misunderstandings or misconceptions are first identified by the teacher. Of course, there are numerous opportunities for students who have been exposed to misconception analysis to use the technique on their own and with peers as they identify topics that need clarification.

Based on her checks of understanding, Colleen Crawford knew that her 5th graders believed that stars and constellations appeared in the same place in the sky every night. In effect, they had overgeneralized information about the North

Star that they had learned in the social studies unit on the Underground Railroad. Ms. Crawford provided small groups of students with different informational text sources about the night sky. Students were asked to read and discuss the information in their texts. Ms. Crawford asked a number of questions of each group that were specific to the texts the group was reading. Then she asked the whole class the big question: "What does your source say about star movement?" As each group searched for this information, Ms. Crawford visited different groups and asked clarifying questions. As each group reported what their text sources said about the movement of stars over time, Ms. Crawford began asking other students to repeat the information and to confirm that their source said the same thing. After each group had discussed their response, Ms. Crawford noted, "We know that we can't believe everything we read and that we should always read critically. But what happens to our understanding when text after text—Web pages, textbooks, trade books, newspaper articles—all report the same thing? Should we change our understanding? Should we assume that there are lots of stars and constellations that move and appear in different places at different times of the year?"

U.S. history teacher Ted Clausen was discussing presidents of the United States with his students. The conversation ebbed and flowed in a highly interactive and engaging way. They had read from a variety of sources and were taking notes from the discussion using graphic organizers. At one point in the discussion, a student said, "You said Roosevelt was president, but he wasn't elected." Mr. Clausen replied, "Yes, in 1901, Theodore Roosevelt was president of the United States, but he wasn't elected to that position. How might that happen? Talk in your groups." After a few minutes, several groups had ideas. One group posited that he was appointed, to which Mr. Clausen responded, "No, we've only had one appointed president and it was George W. Bush." After more discussion, a group said, "Maybe the president died and Roosevelt was vice president and took over?"

Mr. Clausen excitedly responded, "Yes, exactly. Who was that person? The president who died? Well, actually, was assassinated?" After a long pause, Mr. Clausen added, "His first name was William." Michael's hand shot up and he said, with great earnestness, "Shakespeare!" Mr. Clausen replied, "I appreciate your effort, but that's not the right person. Groups, let's explore why that could not be the right answer." After a few minutes, Mr. Clausen asked groups for their responses, which included the following:

- Shakespeare was British, so he couldn't be president of the United States.
- Shakespeare lived hundreds of years ago, long before there was a United States.
- Shakespeare was famous for being an author, not a president.

Through his checking for understanding and the trust he created in the classroom, Mr. Clausen ensured that misconceptions were analyzed and clarified. He knew that his students could identify the reasons that answer was incorrect. But more importantly, he created an environment in which students could analyze incorrect answers for misconceptions. As Michael said afterward, "It's okay to answer in his class 'cuz you get to talk about the answers and figure out why they're right or not. Everybody learns; nobody has to get uptight about it."

Whip Around

The whip around is a useful instructional tool teachers can use to check for understanding in a group setting. While the whip around may not provide individual, student-level information about understanding, it is useful in helping teachers determine if they need to reteach content to the group. As such, the whip around is often used as a closure activity at the end of a period of instruction.

The procedure is fairly simple. First, the teacher poses a question or a task; typically, students are asked to make a list of at least three items. Students then individually respond on a scrap piece of paper. When they have done so, students stand up. The teacher then randomly calls on a student to share one of his or her ideas from the paper. Students check off any items that are said by another student and sit down when all of their ideas have been shared with the group, whether or not they were the one to share them. The teacher continues to call on students until they are all seated. As the teacher listens to the ideas or information shared by students, he or she can determine if there is a general level of understanding or if there are gaps in students' thinking.

Third grade teacher Mandi Smith uses the whip around technique as her daily closure activity. During her unit of study on insects, she asked her students to make a list of the characteristics that distinguish insects from other creatures on Earth. She said that she has to be very specific or her 3rd graders will write comparisons with dinosaurs, space people, and other things not found on Earth. As they completed their whip around, Ms. Smith was pleased to learn that the vast majority of her students understood that insects have three body parts, the head, abdomen, and thorax; that insects have eyes and one pair of antennae and mouthparts; that they all have six legs; that their skeleton is an exoskeleton; and that they have an open circulatory system. Ms. Smith noted, however, that the students did not discuss wings, what the antennae do, or how the mouthparts and legs have adapted. She knew that she would need to review this information the following day to ensure that her students grasped it.

Similarly, health educator Stacey Everson uses a whip around at the end of her classroom discussions. During a 9th grade health education lesson, Ms. Everson asked students to identify the risk factors for suicide. After writing individually for several minutes, the students stood up, and Ms. Everson invited them to share one at a time. She analyzed their responses and noted the factors that most students had on their own pages. She also noted areas that were not addressed by students and provided the class with supplemental readings on the topic as well as a yellow ribbon card (see www.yellowribbon.org for details), which provides students with permission to ask for help as well as tells them what to do if someone else uses the help card.

Conclusion

There are a number of ways that teachers can use oral language—speaking and listening—to check for understanding. Through careful planning and analysis of student responses, teachers can close the gap between what students need to know and what they already know.

3

Using Questions to Check for Understanding

The art of questioning is central to the practice of teaching. Spending a few minutes watching a small child play school gives evidence: the stuffed animals are arranged in rows as the teacher faces them, firing questions all the while. "What's 2+2?" she asks a teddy bear. "Right!" she exclaims to the answer that only she can hear. Even at an early age, children are socialized to a framework of school that demands that the teacher ask questions and the students answer them.

As such, well-crafted questions are a great way for teachers to determine what their students know, need to know, and misunderstand. In this chapter, we explore using questioning to check for understanding. We consider effective questioning techniques as well as instructional practices that promote effective questioning. We also discuss ways to reply to incorrect responses to questions and how teachers use the responses they receive from students to determine the next steps to take in their instruction.

Misuses of Questioning in the Classroom

Durkin's (1978) research on classroom practices confirmed that teachers rely primarily on questioning to check for comprehension. As noted in the previous chapter, the difficulty in this approach is that the questioning rarely advances beyond the Initiate-Respond-Evaluate cycle (Cazden, 1988; see Chapter 2). In the hands of less-able teachers, questioning can devolve into interrogation, as students struggle to guess what's in the teacher's head. Fullan, Hill, and Crévola (2006) assert that teachers from 50 years ago could step into the classrooms of today without much difficulty because so little has changed in the design and delivery of lessons. Undoubtedly, the practice of teacher-generated questions to elicit student responses would be among the most familiar of all.

Traditional teacher-generated questioning is problematic for students. As noted in Chapter 1, gender differences in response rates have a negative impact on girls (Sadker, Sadker, & Klein, 1991). In addition, there is evidence that a vocal minority of students dominate classroom conversations and questioning, while less-assertive students rarely participate (Brophy & Evertson, 1974). This not only results in behavioral difficulties and marginalized students, but it affects the ability of the teacher to check for understanding. After all, knowing that six or seven students understand is not the same as knowing that 32 do. Therefore, it is essential to use effective questioning techniques to elicit richer evidence of understanding. These questioning techniques should be coupled with instructional approaches that maximize participation in classroom discourse.

Effective Questioning Techniques

Constructing Effective Questions

Checking for understanding through questioning should not be thought of as a simple two-step process (question and answer) but rather as a complex progression as the teacher formulates and then listens to the response of the learner. In their book *Quality Questioning,* Walsh and Sattes (2005) describe five distinct steps of the questioning process that they use in their professional development activities called Questioning and Understanding to Improve Learning and Thinking (QUILT). The process is described in Figure 3.1.

The first step is to formulate the question. In particular, the teacher must determine the purpose of the question itself. Is it a recognition question to orient students? For example, the 4th grade geography teacher who points to Pennsylvania on a map of the United States and asks, "What's the name of this state?" is asking a recognition question. This allows the teacher to follow up with questions about

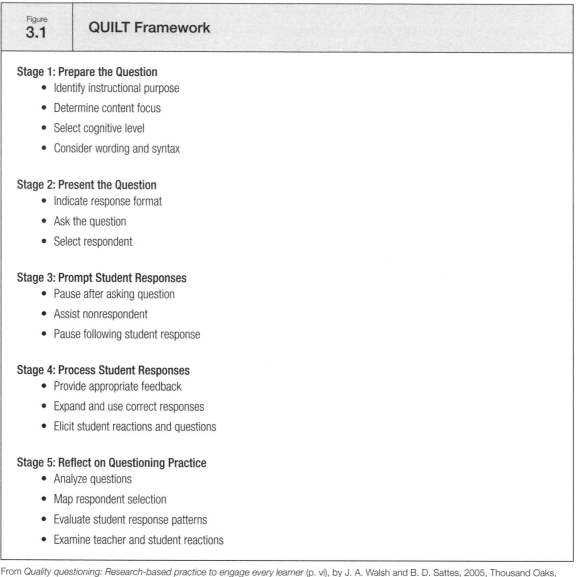

Figure 3.1	**QUILT Framework**

Stage 1: Prepare the Question
- Identify instructional purpose
- Determine content focus
- Select cognitive level
- Consider wording and syntax

Stage 2: Present the Question
- Indicate response format
- Ask the question
- Select respondent

Stage 3: Prompt Student Responses
- Pause after asking question
- Assist nonrespondent
- Pause following student response

Stage 4: Process Student Responses
- Provide appropriate feedback
- Expand and use correct responses
- Elicit student reactions and questions

Stage 5: Reflect on Questioning Practice
- Analyze questions
- Map respondent selection
- Evaluate student response patterns
- Examine teacher and student reactions

From *Quality questioning: Research-based practice to engage every learner* (p. vi), by J. A. Walsh and B. D. Sattes, 2005, Thousand Oaks, CA: Corwin Press.

geographical features of the area, such as its rivers and mountains. A question can also serve the purpose of recalling information, such as when the same geography teacher asks, "What are the two largest cities in Pennsylvania?" In this case, students must recall what they know about the state, about urban centers, and about cities in Pennsylvania. Both questions are examples of factual knowledge but are not likely to promote enduring understanding. It is necessary, however, for students to possess this information. A third type of question asks students to apply information in a novel way. For example, the geography teacher might ask, "What are the advantages and disadvantages of locating the state capital in Harrisburg?" In any case, the teacher needs to be clear on the type of knowledge the question assesses and not fall into the trap of confusing recognition or recall for application.

After formulating the question, the teacher must determine the format of the desired response and who will provide it. Will it be a choral answer, where all students respond together? Is it a partner discussion question? If so, the teacher should preface the question itself with information about the response format so that students know what they will do with the question before it is asked. If it is to be answered by an individual student, teachers should announce the student's name before asking the question. This alerts the learner to the expected response and avoids using the question as a means for classroom management.

Once the question has been asked, students need time to process the answer. Commonly referred to as "wait time," this questioning technique of pausing for three to five seconds allows learners time to digest the question, retrieve information, and formulate a response (Rowe, 1986). This is particularly useful for English language learners who may still be code switching (i.e., mentally translating the question from English to their primary language, then translating their answer to English).

If a student is unable to respond, consider how the question might be scaffolded so that the student can arrive at the correct answer. It is possible that the student does not understand the question itself or that he or she is unable to retrieve the information needed to reply. In designing online learning situations, Dodge (1998) categorizes scaffolds as tools that prompt different types of responses, but we find them to be equally useful in thinking about questioning. Reception scaffolds direct a student to information necessary to formulate an answer. For example, the teacher might prompt the student, "Look at the graph on page 252 of your textbook." Transformation scaffolds provide a way of structuring the information to help students develop an answer. This type of prompt might ask students, "How does the largest bar on the graph on page 252 of your textbook help you to find your answer?" Finally, production scaffolds provide a student with a way of producing an answer. In this case, the teacher might direct the student,

Checking for Understanding

"Use the largest and the smallest bars from the graph on page 252 of your textbook to compare the amounts used."

Once the student has answered, the teacher must use the response to make decisions about what will occur next. Feedback, which includes praise, should be offered to the student; it may include affirmation of a correct response or elaboration on an incomplete answer. It is useful to think about reception, transformation, and production scaffolds as follow-up probes when responding to incomplete or incorrect answers. These follow-up probes serve as a means for teaching students how to use information to formulate answers. Ultimately, the art and science of teaching require the ability to use scaffolds effectively to cultivate student learning. The challenge is to use the right scaffold to assist the learner in doing the cognitive work (Wood, Bruner, & Ross, 1976).

Walsh and Sattes (2005) advise that the final step to effective questioning involves analyzing the techniques used as well as the content of the students' answers. One tool to determine equitable distribution of questions is charting who answers and how often. We have done this using a seating chart inside a clear binder sleeve. As students answer, we place a check on the chart using an overhead marker. This is also useful for identifying students who are not participating. Using this technique may identify patterns such as favoring one section of the room over another or calling on boys more frequently than girls. The content of the questions is important, too, and an audiotape of a lesson can assist in determining whether the range of questions a teacher asks reflects the types of knowledge taught.

Perhaps the most important practice is analyzing students' responses. Again, an audiotape can be useful for engaging in this reflective practice. It is easy to be lured into thinking of students' answers as dichotomous—either correct or incorrect. However, it is essential to keep in mind that a student's answer reflects everything he or she knows and does not know at that particular moment. In other words, an incorrect answer is completely logical to the learner, even if it seems irrational to the teacher. The challenge is to analyze the incorrect answer to hypothesize what the student understands and does not understand, because then the teacher can determine what needs to occur next.

As you listen to a tape of one of your lessons, note the answers your students supplied and how you handled incorrect responses. How often did you scaffold their answers? Were there times when you rephrased a question to clarify understanding?

Were there times when a clue would have been more useful? Sometimes a student is not able to answer even when supports have been offered. In this case, it may be wise to ask another student the question and then return to the first student to ensure understanding. These strategies for responding to incorrect answers are described in Figure 3.2.

Figure 3.2	Helping Students Who Respond Incorrectly

Cue: Use symbols, words, or phrases to help student recall.

Clue: Use overt reminders such as "Starts with . . ."

Probe: Look for reasoning behind an incorrect response or ask for clarity when the response is incomplete.

Rephrase: Pose the same question in different words.

Redirect: Pose the same question to a different student.

Hold accountable later: Later in the lesson, check back with the student who responded incorrectly to make sure that he or she has the correct answer.

From *Quality questioning: Research-based practice to engage every learner* (p. 89), by J. A. Walsh and B. D. Sattes, 2005, Thousand Oaks, CA: Corwin Press. Reprinted with permission. Visit Corwin Press at www.CorwinPress.com.

Providing Nonverbal Support

In addition to the dialogic support teachers offer in helping their students construct answers, nonverbal cues can promote or discourage learner response. You have probably been asked a question by someone and started to respond, only to find that he or she does not appear to be listening to your reply. The person may be looking over your shoulder or may turn away from you to complete a task. It's likely that you immediately thought, "Now, why did he even bother to ask?" It is also likely that you were not inclined to continue the conversation. This type of interaction occurs in classrooms each day. Busy teachers attempt to multitask, posing a question while distributing papers. Or another student catches the teacher's eye, and she turns her back on the student who is attempting to offer a reply. This is usually inadvertent, and yet the effect is the same: "Why did she bother to ask?" Of even more concern, the student may think, "I won't bother to answer again."

Nonverbal cues convey a tone of respect for the respondent and encourage the target student and others to continue to participate. Kindsvatter, Wilen, and Ishler (1996) identify seven components of listening that teachers can and should use to communicate with students that their ideas and participation are valued. They suggest that these seven components indicate to students that the adult is interested and that the student is worthy of attention:

- *Eye contact.* Look directly at the speaker and maintain eye contact.
- *Facial expressions.* Use a variety of appropriate facial expressions, such as smiling or demonstrating surprise or excitement.
- *Body posture.* Use gestures such as hand signals; maintain body posture that signifies openness to students' ideas.
- *Physical distance.* Adjust your position in the classroom according to your condition of instruction; for example, move closer to a student who is speaking (or to a student who is less engaged).
- *Silence.* Be quiet while a student is speaking; don't interrupt; honor wait times after a student stops speaking.
- *Verbal acknowledgments.* Use brief, appropriate verbal acknowledgments such as "Go ahead," "Yes," or "I understand."
- *Subsummaries.* Restate or paraphrase the main ideas presented by students during lengthy discussions.

These simple techniques convey respect for the speaker and provide the questioner with the opportunity to analyze the response and make decisions about scaffolds and feedback. By attending to the respondent and the response, the answer can be used as a means to check for understanding. A distracted teacher is incapable of engaging in anything beyond a superficial awareness of whether the answer was correct or incorrect.

Developing Authentic Questions

As we have noted, teachers are going to ask questions of students. Questions are a great way of checking for understanding. The important thing is to ensure that the questions engage students in deeper thinking and not merely prompt them to recall information that they have read or been told.

One way to make certain that the questions we ask engage students' creative and critical thinking is to plan them in advance using an organizational structure such as Bloom's (1956) taxonomy. Figure 3.3 provides a review of Bloom's taxonomy and descriptive words and prompts related to each level. It is important to keep in mind that a taxonomy is not a hierarchy, and that Bloom never discussed so-called "lower order" and "higher order" questions. Rather, a taxonomy is a way of classifying information, in this case, types of knowledge. Therefore, knowledge and comprehension questions are directed at gathering a specific type of input. This information is necessary to apply, analyze, synthesize, and evaluate. The criticism of knowledge and comprehension questions concerns the extent to which they are used at the expense of others. As we discussed earlier, recognition and recall are requisite skills, but they do not encompass the limits of understanding. Bloom's taxonomy is an excellent tool for developing questions that represent the range of knowledge that should be taught in the classroom.

Sixth grade teacher Alexandria Ollendorff uses Bloom's taxonomy with her students to encourage them to ask and answer their own questions. She introduces prompts like the ones listed in Figure 3.3 to guide her students. They play a daily game in which groups of students create questions based on the information they are studying that day. The questions they create are used for a Jeopardy-type game, with the number of points determined by the level of the question according to the taxonomy (knowledge is 1 point; evaluation is 6 points). During a unit of study about ancient Egypt and their gods, some of the questions one group created included the following:

- Who was Ra? (knowledge)
- Why do some gods and goddesses have animal heads? (comprehension)
- How do you feel about mummification? (evaluation)
- Compare and contrast Isis, Ptah, and Horus in terms of their importance to the Egyptian people. (analysis)
- What role should gods play in setting rules for people? (evaluation)

This process allows the teacher to check for understanding twice—as students create their questions and when they play the game.

Second grade teacher Heather Jennison also uses Bloom's taxonomy in her planning. For example, during her interactive read-aloud of *Nana Upstairs and Nana Downstairs* (dePaola, 1973), Ms. Jennison prepared the following questions:

- *Knowledge:* What were the names Tommy used for his grandmother and great-grandmother?
- *Comprehension:* How did Tommy feel when he went to visit them each Sunday?

	Level	Key Words	Prompts
Figure **3.3**	**Bloom's Taxonomy**		
	Knowledge: Recall data or information.	define, describe, identify, know, label, list, match, name, outline, recall, recognize, reproduce, select, state	Where is . . . What did . . . Who was . . . When did . . . How many . . . Locate it in the story . . . Point to the . . .
	Comprehension: Understand the meaning, translation, interpolation, and interpretation of instructions and problems.	comprehend, convert, defend, distinguish, estimate, explain, extend, generalize, give examples, infer, interpret, paraphrase, predict, rewrite, summarize, translate	Tell me in your own words . . . What does it mean . . . Give me an example of . . . Describe what . . . Illustrate the part of the story that . . . Make a map of . . . What is the main idea of . . .
	Application: Use a concept in a new situation or unprompted use of an abstraction.	apply, change, compute, construct, demonstrate, discover, manipulate, modify, operate, predict, prepare, produce, relate, show, solve, use	What would happen to you if . . . Would you have done the same as . . . If you were there, would you . . . How would you solve the problem . . . In the library, find information about . . .
	Analysis: Separate material or concepts into component parts so that its organizational structure may be understood.	analyze, break down, compare, contrast, diagram, deconstruct, differentiate, discriminate, distinguish, identify, illustrate, infer, outline, relate, select, separate	What things would you have used . . . What other ways could . . . What things are similar/different? What part of this story was the most exciting? What things couldn't have happened in real life? What kind of person is . . . What caused _____ to act the way he/she did?

- *Application:* What would you have said to Tommy's older brother when he called Nana Upstairs "a witch"?
- *Analysis:* How were Nana Upstairs and Nana Downstairs alike and different?
- *Synthesis:* Add a new last page to the book. What might the two grandmothers say to the adult Tommy when he looks at the stars to remember them?
- *Evaluation:* Did you like this story? Why or why not?

Figure 3.3	Bloom's Taxonomy (continued)	
Level	**Key Words**	**Prompts**
Synthesis: Build a structure or pattern from diverse elements. Put parts together to form a whole, with emphasis on creating a new meaning or structure.	categorize, combine, compile, compose, create, devise, design, explain, generate, modify, organize, plan, rearrange, reconstruct, relate, reorganize, revise, rewrite, summarize, tell, write	What would it be like if . . . What would it be like to live . . . Design a . . . Pretend you are a . . . What would have happened if . . . Why/why not? Use your imagination to draw a picture of . . . Add a new item on your own . . . Tell/write a different ending . . .
Evaluation: Make judgments about the value of ideas or materials.	appraise, compare, conclude, contrast, criticize, critique, defend, describe, discriminate, evaluate, explain, interpret, justify, relate, summarize, support	Would you recommend this book? Why or why not? Select the best . . . Why is it the best? What do you think will happen to . . . Why do you think that? Could this story really have happened? Which character would you most like to meet? Was _____ good or bad? Why? Did you like the story? Why?

While Bloom's taxonomy provides us with a way of organizing questions, teachers can structure interesting questions in other ways. The goal is for questions to provide students with an opportunity to think and the teacher with an opportunity to check for understanding. Figure 3.4 provides a list of question stems that teachers can use in planning open-ended questions.

Instructional Practices That Promote Participation

In addition to monitoring nonverbal behavior and creating quality questions, there are a number of instructional practices that teachers can use to increase participation and engagement in the classroom. The following strategies are especially useful in the area of questioning and may also apply to other methods of checking for understanding.

Figure 3.4	Sample Question Stems

- How is _____ similar to/different from _____?
- What are the characteristics/parts of _____?
- In what other way might we show/illustrate_____?
- What is the big idea/key concept in _____?
- How does _____ relate to _____?
- What ideas/details can you add to _____?
- Give an example of _____.
- What is wrong with _____?
- What might you infer from _____?
- What conclusions might be drawn from _____?
- What questions are we trying to answer? What problem are we trying to solve?
- What are you assuming about _____?
- What might happen if _____?
- What criteria might you use to judge/evaluate _____?
- What evidence supports _____?
- How might we prove/confirm _____?
- How might this be viewed from the perspective of _____?
- What alternatives should be considered?
- What approach/strategy could you use to _____?
- How else might you say _____?

Adapted from *Understanding by design* (p. 167), by G. Wiggins and J. McTighe, 1998, Alexandria, VA: Association for Supervision and Curriculum Development.

Response Cards

Response cards are index cards, signs, dry-erase boards, magnetic boards, or other items that are simultaneously held up by all students in class to indicate their response to a question or problem presented by the teacher. Using response cards, the teacher can easily note the responses of individual students while teaching the whole group. Additionally, response cards allow for participation by the whole class and not just a few students who raise their hands to respond (Heward et al., 1996).

While there are a number of examples of response cards, there are basically two types: preprinted and write-on cards. Preprinted cards already have responses on them; write-on cards allow students to indicate their responses in real time. There are specific reasons to use each.

When Dana Nielsen wanted her 1st grade students to learn to use response cards, she first provided each student with two preprinted index cards that read "yes" and "no." Then, she introduced the picture book *George and Martha* (Marshall, 1974). Looking at the cover, she asked her students, "Are these dogs?" Several hands shot up; Alicia shouted out, "NO!" Ms. Nielsen paused and looked at the class. She reminded them that they should use their response cards and asked the question again. This time, all of the students held up their "no" cards. Ms. Nielsen then asked, "Is this story a real story? Do you think it could really happen?" Most of the class held up their "no" cards, but four held up "yes" cards. Ms. Nielsen said, "Hmm, I wonder if these animals really are friends and would wear clothes like this." She then pointed to the name of the author, read it aloud, and asked, "Is this the name of the author?" All of the "yes" cards were displayed. Ms. Nielsen was quite pleased to see this as she had been focusing her instruction on identifying title and author information. As she read the book, she paused periodically to ask questions. At one point she asked, "Do you think Martha likes split pea soup?" About half of the "yes" cards went up. She asked Jeremy why he held up his "yes" card, and he answered, "Because she likes to make it. See right there? She likes to cook that." Ms. Nielsen then asked Brianna why she held up her "no" card. Brianna replied, "Yuck, peas! She can't like that." The use of these preprinted response cards ensured that all of the students remained focused on the contents of the book and allowed Ms. Nielsen to check her students' understanding of the information on a regular basis.

Mr. Hernandez uses response cards with his 3rd grade students during their word study lessons. He purchased tile board (used in shower stalls) from his local hardware store and had it cut into 12-inch squares. These work great with dry-erase pens as low-cost personal write-on, wipe-off boards.

Mr. Hernandez displayed a bunch of scrambled letters (d, s, i, a, n, u, o, r) on the overhead projector. Students were asked to write three-letter words using these letters and hold up their boards. The range of student responses included *nor, our, sin, sun, son, and, run, ran,* and *dor.* (Mr. Hernandez noted that Tony had incorrectly spelled *door* as *dor.*) Then Mr. Hernandez asked students to create four-letter words using these letters. The range of words now included *rain, dino, sour, sins, said, raid,* and so on. These write-on response cards allowed Mr. Hernandez to check his students' understanding of word study while his students identified longer and longer words from the letters that eventually formed the word *dinosaur.*

Physics teacher Tom Jensen uses preprinted response cards that read "potential energy" and "kinetic energy" as part of his instruction in matter and motion. Using an LCD projector to display images on the screen, Mr. Jensen asked his students to identify if the energy being displayed was potential or kinetic. In response to a slide showing a stretched rubber band, all of the students held up their "potential energy" cards. To a slide of a pitcher throwing a baseball, all but two students held up their "kinetic energy" cards. Additional slides focused on roller coasters, a professional runner, a glass of water at the edge of a dinner table, and so on. Several slides later, the image of a massive waterfall was displayed. The majority of the students held up their "kinetic energy" cards. Mr. Jensen asked Antony why he held up his "potential energy" card. Antony responded, "I see more potential energy. Look at all that water ready to go over the edge. The majority of the information in this picture suggests potential; only a small amount of the water is really kinetic at any one time." Mr. Jensen's use of response cards allowed him to check his students' understanding of the key ideas they were learning. These cards also allowed him to note areas of weakness or misconceptions that he could address in his subsequent instruction.

Hand Signals

Hand signals are often used as a classroom management tool. For example, Wong and Wong (2005) suggest a classroom procedure called "Give Me Five" in which students are taught specific behavioral expectations for each of the numbers 5, 4, 3, 2, and 1 as the teacher counts down on his or her fingers. Hand signals have also been successfully used to ensure that students with ADD/ADHD or behavioral disabilities get immediate and private feedback from their teachers (and possibly trusted peers) regarding their performance.

Students can also use hand signals to indicate their understanding of content information. Similar to response cards, hand signals require engagement from the whole group and allow the teacher to check for understanding in large groups of students.

In her kindergarten classroom, Donna Kim uses "thumbs up" to check her students' understanding of instructions and information. Her students know how to display the following signals:

- *Thumbs up:* "I understand _____ and can explain it."
- *Thumbs sideways:* "I'm not completely sure about _____."
- *Thumbs down:* "I do not yet understand _____."

At one point, Ms. Kim used the "thumbs up" procedure to determine which of her students needed additional assistance in their journal writing. The task involved writing at least two follow-up sentences and drawing an illustration of kangaroos based on a shared reading and interactive writing lesson the class had just completed. Ms. Kim reminded her students that the sentences needed to be informational and not fiction. She then said, "Thumbs up?" Several students immediately put their thumbs up and were dismissed to their tables. A few students had their thumbs sideways, and three had their thumbs down. Ms. Kim started with Creshena, who had her thumb sideways. Creshena asked, "You mean it could really happen, right?" Ms. Kim replied, "Yes, informational—not fiction or pretend." When all of the students who had their thumbs sideways had their questions answered and were sitting at their desks writing and illustrating, Ms. Kim focused on the students with their thumbs down. She reviewed the shared reading text, thinking aloud about the range of possible sentences that her students might want to write.

Using this procedure, Ms. Kim was able to allocate instructional time to students who really needed additional support to be successful. In addition, her ability to check for understanding ensured that her students were successful in completing the task at hand.

Seventh grade pre-algebra teacher Tara Jacobsen also uses hand signals to check her students' understanding. As she models the solutions to word problems, she asks her students to hold up fingers based on how well they understand each step along the way. Five fingers means that you have a deep understanding and can explain this step or idea to others in the class; one finger means that you have no idea what just happened. Two to four fingers indicate varying levels of understanding.

As Ms. Jacobsen worked out a problem on the overhead, she shared her thinking and checked for understanding regularly. The problem read as follows:

An 800-seat multiplex is divided into three theaters. There are 270 seats in Theater 1, and there are 150 more seats in Theater 2 than in Theater 3. How many seats are in Theater 2?

Ms. Jacobsen: Okay, so my total has to equal 800; that's all the seats we have in the whole thing. Fingers?

All hands are showing five fingers.

Ms. Jacobsen: I know that there are 270 seats exactly in Theater 1. Fingers?

All hands show five fingers.

Ms. Jacobsen: Well, that's not a lot of help yet. We need to know how many are in Theater 2. There are 150 more seats in Theater 2 than in Theater 3. Thoughts?

Almost all hands show five fingers; three students show three or four.

Ms. Jacobsen: Let me think about this again. [She underlines "150 more seats."] There are 150 more seats in Theater 2 than in Theater 3. So I know that Theater 2 has to be bigger than Theater 3 by 150 seats. Responses?

All hands again show five fingers.

Ms. Jacobsen: So, if Theater 3 is represented as x, then Theater 2 can be represented as $x + 150$, because there are 150 more seats in Theater 2 than 3. Fingers?

All hands show five fingers.

Ms. Jacobsen: I know that all three theaters have to add up to 800. T1 + T2 + T3 = 800. Reactions?

All hands show five fingers.

Ms. Jacobsen: I know that T1 is 270. Fingers?

All hands show five fingers.

Ms. Jacobsen: I know that T2 is $x + 150$. Thoughts?

All hands show five fingers.

Ms. Jacobsen: I know that T3 is x. Fingers?

All hands show five fingers.

Ms. Jacobsen: So, my formula is $270 + (x + 150) + x = 800$. Do you agree?

All hands show five fingers.

Ms. Jacobsen: So I can add like terms: $420 + 2x = 800$. Fingers?

Many hands show four fingers; several students show one or two.

Ms. Jacobsen: Oh, so here's the problem. We need to think about adding like terms. Talk with your partner and explain how like terms are added. [Students start talking with one another.]

Ms. Jacobsen: Here's how I did this. I added the numbers together: $270 + 150 = 420$. There isn't a multiplication sign to confuse us; we can just add. Fingers?

All hands show five fingers.

Ms. Jacobsen: Then I added x and x together. Is this what you talked about with your partners? Mikel, what did your partner tell you?

Mikel: She said that the two unknowns could be added because they were both the same kind—x.

Ms. Jacobsen: Right. Are you all thinking that? Do you agree?

All hands show five fingers.

Ms. Jacobsen: Now, I just need to solve for the x. That's the simple part, right? So my answer is 190. Thoughts?

All hands show five fingers.

Ms. Jacobsen: But let's check our variables. We let x = Theater 3. Remember that we were asked to find out how many seats were in Theater 2. So we have to return to our variables and remember that Theater 2 is $x + 150$. So Theater 2, my answer, is 340. Fingers?

All hands show five fingers.

Ms. Jacobsen: Let's check to see if this works. We know that Theater 1 has 270 seats. We learned that Theater 3 has 190. We know that Theater 2, from our addition, has 340 seats. So let's add those together. Do we get 800? Fingers?

All hands show five fingers.

The use of hand signals allowed Ms. Jacobsen to identify the places where her students did not understand the math content so that she could reteach this information on the spot. Checking for understanding as she modeled the solution to the word problem increased the likelihood that her students could use this information to solve similar problems in small groups and eventually on their own.

Audience Response Systems

New technologies have provided teachers with unique opportunities for checking for understanding. For example, Audience Response Systems (ARS)—handheld devices (e.g., remote controls) that allow each learner to respond to questions individually—enable teachers to gather students' responses to interactive questions in real time. Most systems of this type are integrated into software programs such as PowerPoint so that the responses are aggregated and displayed immediately. Imagine being a learner in a classroom where you used a remote control to answer questions, knowing that your response would matter each and every time.

Tom Hayden uses an ARS from TurningPoint (www.turningtechnologies.com) to engage his middle school science students during their unit of study on cells. At one point, he asked the following question:

Which of these things do both plant and animal cells have?
A. Cytoplasm
B. Chloroplasts
C. Cell wall
D. Vacuole

Students quickly entered their responses on their handheld devices. Over 90 percent of the students had this answer correct. Mr. Hayden congratulated his students and quickly summarized the answer: "Yep, cytoplasm. Both animal and plant cells have cytoplasm. You'll recall that cytoplasm is jellylike material that fills cells."

Pleased that his students knew this, he continued to ask questions, provide answers, and integrate brief lecture points into this experience with his students. They remained engaged, waiting for opportunities to demonstrate their knowledge of science. This changed when he asked the following question:

What is the function of the cell membrane?
A. To control which substances move in and out of the cell
B. To help the cell maintain a firm shape
C. To make food for the cell
D. All of the above

More than half of the students selected D; the other half were spread across answers A, B, and C. Mr. Hayden was clearly surprised. "Wow!" he responded: "That membrane really caught us! Why does the cell have a membrane? Let's look at this illustration again. [He turned on the overhead projector and displayed a diagram of a cell.] Tell your partner how the cell maintains its shape. [He paused while students talked.] Ah yes, I'm hearing the answer all around. The cell *wall* helps the cell maintain its shape. So B can't be correct. Try again, everyone. [Students reentered their responses on the handheld devices.] Oh, I'm glad to see no one selected B and only a few people selected C, but lots of you selected D. How could that be if we just determined that B can't be correct? If B isn't correct, then D can't be your answer. Let's review some test-taking skills . . ."

Using technology, questions, and systems for checking for understanding, Mr. Hayden was able to challenge his students' knowledge and misconceptions and provide them with a strong foundation in understanding the physical and biological world.

ReQuest

ReQuest, or reciprocal questioning (Manzo, 1969), was designed to teach students to ask and answer questions as they read. We know that good readers engage in questioning as they read, and the theory is that teaching all students to do this will improve their comprehension (Harvey & Goudvis, 2000). In fact, simply thinking about questions while reading improves comprehension, whether the questions are "question-the-author" questions, "question–answer relationship" questions, or dense questions (Beck, McKeown, Hamilton, & Kucan, 1997; Christenbury, 2006; Raphael, Highfield, & Au, 2006).

The original version of ReQuest requires that the teacher lead the whole class in silently reading a segment of text. Students then ask questions of the teacher about the content of the section of text they read. Next, students and teacher change roles. They all read the next section of the text silently. When they finish the second segment of text, the teacher questions the students. They take turns back and forth alternating between questioning and responding. As the ReQuest process continues, students learn to imitate the teacher's questioning behavior.

Physics teacher Vince Andrews uses ReQuest in his classroom on a weekly basis. He starts each term modeling ReQuest with his students as outlined above. Over time, he transfers the responsibility totally to his students. They work in pairs, taking turns responding and questioning as they read complex pieces of text. In one instance, students focused on an online text about amusement park physics (www.learner.org/exhibits/parkphysics/index.html). After reading, pairs of students asked and answered questions about roller coasters, how they work, how mass has an impact on the ride, and so on. After reading the section "Wooden or Steel Coaster: Does It Make a Difference?" one student, Violet, asked the following questions:

- What role does the construction material play in the ride?
- What are the advantages and disadvantages of each type of coaster?
- Which would you rather ride and why?
- Which do you think is safer and why?

Socratic Seminar

The Greek philosopher and teacher Socrates (ca. 470–399 BCE) was convinced that the way to gain reliable knowledge was through the practice of disciplined conversation. He called this method *dialectic,* which means the art or practice of examining opinions or ideas logically, often by the method of question and answer, so as to determine their validity.

Educators have developed the Socratic seminar as a way of engaging a group of learners in a conversation and series of questions. There are a number of considerations to address when conducting Socratic seminars, including the text, the question, the leader, and the participants.

The text. Socratic seminar texts should be selected for their ability to engage students in discussion. The text should be rich enough to ensure that readers will ask and answer questions for themselves. Both narrative and informational texts can be used in Socratic seminars. The most important thing is that the text can capture the imagination of the group.

The question. A Socratic seminar begins with a question posed by the leader. As students develop their expertise in Socratic seminars, they will begin asking questions themselves. The question should have no right answer. Instead, the question should reflect authentic wonder and interest. A good opening question requires that students return to the text to think, search, evaluate, wonder, or infer. Responses to the opening question should generate new questions, leading to new responses and still more questions. In a Socratic seminar, inquiry is natural and continuous.

The leader. In a Socratic seminar, the leader serves as both participant in and facilitator of the discussion. The seminar leader demonstrates "habits of mind" (see Costa & Kallick, 2000) that lead to a reflective and thoughtful exploration of the ideas presented in the text and referenced in the discussion. In addition to this facilitator role, the leader is also a seminar participant. As such, the leader actively takes part in the group's examination of the text. Naturally, the leader must know the text well enough to anticipate misconceptions and misunderstandings, various interpretations, reader responses, and issues that may invoke strong emotions. At the same time, the leader must trust the process and allow the group to come to its own understanding of the text and the ideas represented in the text.

The participants. In a Socratic seminar, participants are responsible for the quality of the seminar and discussion. Good seminars result when participants study the text in advance; listen actively; share their ideas, opinions, and questions; and search for evidence in the text to support their ideas. Over time, participants realize that the leader is not expecting "right answers" to the questions that are asked but instead is hoping to get students to think out loud as they discover the excitement of exploring important issues through shared inquiry. Guidelines for Socratic seminar participants can be found in Figure 3.5.

Figure 3.5	Guidelines for Participants in a Socratic Seminar

1. Refer to the text when needed during the discussion. A seminar is not a test of memory. You are not "learning a subject"; your goal is to understand the ideas, issues, and values reflected in the text.
2. It's okay to "pass" when asked to contribute.
3. Do not participate if you are not prepared. A seminar should not be a bull session.
4. Do not stay confused; ask for clarification.
5. Stick to the point currently under discussion; make notes about ideas you want to come back to.
6. Don't raise hands; take turns speaking.
7. Listen carefully.
8. Speak up so that all can hear you.
9. Talk to each other, not just to the leader or teacher.
10. Discuss ideas rather than each other's opinions.
11. You are responsible for the seminar, even if you don't know it or admit it.

From *Guidelines for participants in a Socratic seminar,* by C. Adams, 2004, Vestavia Hills High School, Birmingham, Alabama.

Conclusion

Questioning is a powerful tool that teachers can use to engage students in authentic learning. Questioning is also an excellent way for teachers to check for understanding. There are a number of effective approaches to questioning, both at the individual level and at the classroom level. However, questions can be ineffective when they are not thoughtfully planned or when a teacher's nonverbal behavior indicates lack of interest in the responses or the individual responding.

4

Using Writing to Check for Understanding

It is said that children spend their first years learning how to read and then the remainder of their lives reading to learn. Using writing as a mechanism for learning is not often discussed by parents and teachers. Yet writing offers an excellent pathway for brainstorming, clarifying, and questioning. There is evidence of increased student performance when writing is used as a tool for thinking in high school algebra (Miller & England, 1989), middle school science (Keys, 1999), family and consumer sciences (Bye & Johnson, 2004), and elementary social studies (Brophy, 1990). Nevertheless, despite all the known benefits of using writing to learn content, we rarely think of writing as a way for us to learn about our students' thinking.

Writing clarifies thinking. For that matter, writing *is* thinking. Analyzing student writing is a great way for teachers to determine what their students know. In this chapter, we explore the use of writing to check for understanding. We consider various writing prompts and how teachers can use the writing they receive from students to determine the next steps to take in their instruction. This chapter focuses on the use of writing across the curriculum as an assessment tool and not the teaching of writing for writing's sake. Elbow (1994) describes two purposes for writing:

It is helpful to distinguish between two very different goals for writing. The normal and conventional goal is writing to demonstrate learning: for this goal the writing should be good—it should be clear and, well . . . right. It is high stakes writing. We all know and value this kind of writing so I don't need to argue for it here, but let me give one more reason why it's important: if we don't ask students to demonstrate their learning in essays and essay exams, we are likely to grade unfairly because of being misled about how much they have learned in our course. Students often seem to know things on short-answer or multiple-choice tests that they don't really understand.

But there is another important kind of writing that is less commonly used and valued, and so I want to stress it here: writing for learning. This is low stakes writing. The goal isn't so much good writing as coming to learn, understand, remember and figure out what you don't yet know. Even though low stakes writing-to-learn is not always good as writing, it is particularly effective at promoting learning and involvement in course material, and it is much easier on teachers—especially those who aren't writing teachers. (p. 1)

It is Elbow's second purpose that is the focus of this chapter. Writing to learn is a powerful tool for students. It helps them clarify their thinking and their understanding. Along the way, writing allows teachers to check for understanding. Figure 4.1 contains a list of general recommendations useful in developing prompts for writing to learn. Keep these guidelines in mind as you consider the examples in this chapter.

Why Use Writing as an Assessment Tool?

The National Assessment of Educational Progress (NAEP) framework includes a writing assessment. As the board of governors for NAEP notes, writing is "one of the most important skills that young people can acquire and develop throughout their lives" (National Center for Education Statistics, 2002). The NAEP writing assessment focuses on three areas that are commonly used in classrooms across the country (Persky, Daane, & Jin, 2003):

* *Narrative writing* (telling a story). Writers incorporate their imagination and creativity in the production of stories or personal essays.

Figure 4.1	General Principles for Creating Good Writing-to-Learn Assignments

- Articulate the desired learning and thinking precisely: "The purpose of this assignment is for you to apply spectrum analysis techniques to a specific star you choose to study" (astronomy); "Describe a Jungian archetype present in your favorite TV show" (psychology); "Paraphrase the key assertion in Chapter 3."

- Provide genre and format constraints: "Write one coherent paragraph"; "In one page, do two things: find the earliest definition of a key word in the poem and assess that meaning's relevance to the poem as a whole" (English).

- Consider grading writing assignments using a portfolio system, point system, or "check +, check, check −" system. You could also use "primary trait" scoring, grading the paper only on how successfully the student accomplished the learning asked for in the prompt.

- Make assignments short and able to be completed and graded quickly.

- Place assignments strategically in the curriculum to accomplish a specific goal.

- Collect the assignments but don't grade them formally; if you comment, comment on content rather than sentence errors.

- Where appropriate, have students collaborate on assignments or share work they've completed.

- Don't read and comment on everything.

From "Writing for learning and growth," by S. L. Miller., 2006, Sonoma State University Writing Center. Retrieved February 7, 2007, from http://www.sonoma.edu/programs/writingcenter/pdf_files/assignmentsforlearning.pdf

- *Informative writing* (informing the reader). Writers provide the reader with information (e.g., reporting on events or analyzing concepts).

- *Persuasive writing* (persuading the reader). Writers seek to persuade the reader to take action or to bring about change.

These types of writing are commonly taught as genres; therefore, the emphasis is on the form of the piece. Young children develop step-by-step instructions for making a peanut butter and jelly sandwich, with each point in the process numbered in sequence. Older students are instructed to state their position and address counterarguments in order to write a successful persuasive piece. It is less common to analyze the content of the writing itself. For example, what does the informative piece reveal about what the 1st grade student knows and does not know regarding sandwich assembly? How pertinent is the information cited by the 7th grader regarding the debate over school uniforms?

Perhaps the most well publicized example of this phenomenon was the analysis of the results of the first administration of the SAT writing test. Massachusetts Institute of Technology professor Les Perelman analyzed the length and content of the

54 anchor papers, graded essays, and samples released by the publisher of the test and discovered a strong correlation between length and score. "I have never found a quantifiable predictor in 25 years of grading that was anywhere near as strong as this one," he reported: "If you just graded them based on length without ever reading them, you'd be right over 90 percent of the time" (in Winerip, 2005). According to the *New York Times* article, Perelman reported that the scoring manual for the test stated that factual errors were not to be factored into the score for the essay (Winerip, 2005).

Using writing to check for understanding means looking at how the form and the content interact. Since writing is thinking, the message and the way the message is conveyed are interrelated. The execution of the form should support the information being communicated. In this way, the ability to narrate, to inform, or to persuade becomes a mechanism for looking at the ways in which students understand.

Misuses of Writing in the Classroom

The most common misuse of writing in the classroom is using it as part of a classroom management plan. In some places, writing is used as a consequence for problematic behavior. While the days of writing what one won't do over and over have passed (e.g., "I will not pull Susie's hair" 100 times), writing is still used to address a needed correction in behavior. For example, a teacher may require that a student write an explanation about why she was late or why he did not complete his homework. In these situations, there is a telegraphed message to students that writing is neither fun nor something that requires thinking.

Writing has also been used to label and sort students. As the position statement on writing assessments put forth by the National Council of Teachers of English (NCTE) notes, writing assessments "can be used for a variety of appropriate purposes, both inside the classroom and outside: providing assistance to students; awarding a grade; placing students in appropriate courses; allowing them to exit a course or sequence of courses; and certifying proficiency, to name some of the more obvious. But writing assessment can be abused as well." (CCCC Committee on Assessment, 1995, p. 430; see www.ncte.org/about/over/positions/category/write/107610.htm for the full text of NCTE's position statement on writing assessments)

Writing Strategies to Check for Understanding

You can use writing in a number of ways to check for understanding. During language arts instruction, writing can be used to determine the next steps for instruction in topics such as grammar, spelling, and comprehension. During content-area instruction, student writing can be used to determine what students know, what they still need to know, and what they are confused about. As Kuhrt and Farris (1990) remind us, "The upper reaches of Bloom's taxonomy could not be reached without the use of some form of writing" (p. 437).

Interactive Writing

Interactive writing allows students to share the pen with the teacher. This strategy can be used with individual students, small groups, or the whole class. After agreeing on a message orally, students take turns writing on the dry-erase board or on chart paper. The idea is that interactive writing flows "from ideas, to spoken words, to printed messages" (Clay, 2001, p. 27). The procedures are fairly straightforward. First, the writers discuss a topic and agree on a message. This takes ideas and moves them into spoken words. The teacher then asks students to come write a section of the message. This can be a letter, a word, or a phrase. As each writer finishes, the whole group reads the message aloud, both the part already written and the part still in their minds. While each student writes, the teacher provides related instruction to the rest of the class. For example, in a phonics lesson, if a given writer were writing the word *string*, the teacher may ask members of the class to identify other words with the onset pattern *str-* (such as *strong, strain,* or *stripe*). These minilessons extend students' thinking about print and their understandings of the conventions of language and are based on errors, misunderstandings, or next steps for learning that the teacher has identified through checking for understanding (Callella & Jordano, 2002; McCarrier, Pinnell, & Fountas, 2000).

The 2nd graders in Rebecca Fieler's class used interactive writing to create a friendly letter. They had just finished listening to and reading *The Jazz Fly* (Gollub, 2000). As a class, they discussed composing a friendly letter and decided that they would write to the author and tell him that they enjoyed his singing on the CD that accompanies the book, his illustrations, and the funny story about the fly that uses the sounds of other animals to make music for the bugs. One at a time, students wrote on a piece of chart paper.

When Justin approached the chart paper, instead of the word *really,* he wrote *willy.* Ms. Fieler took note of this misunderstanding and responded this way:

Ms. Fieler: Justin, let's take a second look at this word. It's *really.* Let's say the whole sentence again as a class. *We really like your book.* Justin, do you want to change anything?

Justin: Oh, yeah. [Justin returns to the chart paper and uses a large strip of correction tape to change the word to *Reely.*]

Ms. Fieler: Interesting. I know that there are two ways to spell the root word: *real* and *reel.* [Ms. Fieler writes both on the dry-erase board.] *Real* means true or accurate. *Reel* is like a fishing reel or movie projector reel. Which one do you think would be the correct one for *really?*

Justin [hitting his head with his hand]: Oops, I got the wrong one. It should be *real.* [Justin uses the correction tape to change *Reely* to *Realy.*]

Ms. Fieler: Oh, now I see. But when I say "real-ly," do you hear one or two syllables?

Justin: Two. Yeah, two.

Ms. Fieler: Let's think about what we know about double consonants.

Justin: [He pauses.] There's a vowel close by. [Ms. Fieler had taught this mnemonic a few weeks earlier.]

Ms. Fieler: That's right! So what do you want to add?

Justin: Yeah, so it should be *really.* [Justin adds the second *l* to the word.]

Ms. Fieler: You're amazing. I really appreciate your thinking through this word with me. I bet the class appreciates your hard work in making our letter correct. I see how you wrote your word below with an editor's mark. I also see that you used a capital letter to start the word. I think I know why you did that. Is it because it's a new line?

Justin: Yeah. But the word goes there [he points to the space where the incorrect version was], so it should be a small letter. [Justin uses the correction tape to change the letter *R* to lowercase.]

Ms. Fieler: Excellent. Who wants to add the next word in our friendly letter to Mr. Gollub? [Several hands go up.] Andrea, come on up.

Ms. Fieler's interactive instruction continued until the letter was completed. Ms. Fieler then asked the class to write their own friendly letters and used the exercise to check students' understanding of spelling, grammar, and the friendly letter format, all of which are content standards in 2nd grade. Britney's friendly letter to her hamster (seen in Figure 4.2) allowed Ms. Fieler to see that Britney understood the general format of a friendly letter and that she needed continued work on spelling patterns, especially vowel digraphs.

Figure 4.2	Britney's Friendly Letter to Her Hamster

June 5, 2004

Dear Mr. Brownie,
     Please try to slep with your eyes closed. When you have your eys open at night, you see you're whele and want to run. That makes me wake up. I am tired for school and you can slep all the day. Thank you for tring to slep with you're eys closed.

Your friend,
     Britney

Interactive writing can also be used with older students (Fisher & Frey, 2003). While younger students are often eager to jump out of their seats and participate in writing events, older students are usually more reluctant. When teachers use interactive writing to check for understanding with older students, they need to have firmly established routines and the trust of their students.

Brooke Silva is a 9th grade English language development teacher who uses interactive writing in her classroom. She regularly meets with small groups of students based on instructional needs that she has identified in their writing. Amalee, Amor, Jorge, and Tien regularly forget the plural -*s* and possessive -*s* in their speaking and writing. During their small-group meetings, Ms. Silva discusses current events with her students, and they summarize the discussions through interactive writing. Ms. Silva pays close attention to the plural and possessive endings as her instructional focus. During one of the small-group meetings, students were discussing North Korea's test of nuclear missiles. The group agreed on several sentences to write, including, "Testing missiles is dangerous and may not be in the world's best interest." Tien was the first to write, and he correctly wrote the word *Testing* with a capital letter. As he was writing, Ms. Silva asked her students to think about the various uses of the word *testing* and provided a minilesson on words that have multiple meanings. Amalee wrote the next word, *missile*, leaving off the plural -*s*. Ms. Silva paused in the small-group discussion and asked the group to repeat the sentence. She then asked them if the word *missile* was possessive ("Does the missile own something?") or if it was plural ("Is there more than one?"). Through her small-group interactive writing, Ms. Silva is able to determine what her students know about the content—in this case word analysis and vocabulary—and what she still needs to teach, practice, and reinforce.

Read-Write-Pair-Share

Building on the Think-Pair-Share strategy discussed in Chapter 2, Read-Write-Pair-Share focuses on print-based literacy skills while still encouraging partners to discuss and make meaning of content. The procedure is fairly straightforward. Students read (or view, in the case of videos or DVDs) the material, write in response to this information, engage in a partner conversation about what they've read and written, and then share their ideas with the whole class. Along the way, the teacher can check for understanding. For example, the written responses may be a source of information about what students already know or misunderstand. Similarly, listening in on the partner conversations provides the teacher with valuable information about students' thinking.

For example, in Ms. Nelson's 8th grade English class, students read a short story called "Salvador, Late or Early" (Cisneros, 1991), which focuses on a boy who takes care of his younger brother and sisters. Each student was asked to write a personal response to this selection. Kaila's response can be found in Figure 4.3.

Figure 4.3	Kaila's Response to "Salvador, Late or Early"

It's sad. Why doesn't the teacher know his name? Does she not care about him? Is he forgotten? Is it because he has to take care of his brother and sister? I don't have any younger brothers or sisters to take care of, but if I did, I would take care of them. That's what a family should do, they should help out and keep together. Maybe he is happy with his balloons. There's more of them than the sadness.

Next, Ms. Nelson asked her students to turn to their partners and discuss their reactions and comments. As they did so, she walked through the room, listening to conversations and quickly reading the students' written responses. Doing so allowed her to identify key points that she wanted to make with the whole class. In this particular period, a number of students indicated that they thought this story was sad. She wanted them to think about why the story made them sad and decided that this would be a great journal writing prompt as part of her lesson closure. She also noticed that several of her students were applying literal interpretations to figurative language. She made a note to develop some focus lessons on figurative language and to create a writing assignment in which students use figurative language. In response to the assignment, Amalee wrote a poem using figurative language to describe love (see Figure 4.4). Her poem reflects the progress she made in understanding this literary device.

Figure 4.4	Amalee's "Love Is . . ." Poem

Love is . . .
. . . as fragrant as blooming bright flowers, opening slowly with the light of the smiling sun.
. . . as deep as the ocean, burying mysterious memories filled with happiness and sadness.
. . . as soft as a silken scarf that covers my lover's defects.
. . . like a light switch that brightens the chambers of my heart.
. . . as enormous as a mountain, hard to climb but I want to reach its peak.
. . . like the thorns of a rose if you don't take care of it.

Summary Writing

Summary writing is a valuable tool for checking for understanding because it provides the teacher with insight into how learners condense information. It is analogous to retelling (see Chapter 2) and serves as a way for students to demonstrate their ability to recapitulate what they have read, viewed, or done. There is evidence that the act of summarizing new knowledge in written form can lead to higher levels of understanding. Radmacher and Latosi-Sawin (1995) found that college students who wrote summaries as part of their course scored an average of 8 percent higher on their final exam, compared to students who did not write summaries.

The most common form of summary writing is the précis, a short piece that contains the major ideas or concepts of a topic. The emphasis is on an economy of words and an accurate rendering of the read or observed phenomenon. Because it is brief, word choice is critical. The ability to select the word that best represents a concept is reflective of the level of understanding of the topic. Mark Twain, a word master if ever there was one, describes word choice in this way: "The difference between the almost right word and the right word is really a large matter—it's the difference between the lightning bug and the lightning" (in Bainton, 1890). Indeed, the ability to write for accuracy and conciseness is a good indicator of the writer's knowledge of the topic and control over the form. Another Twain quote also applies: "I didn't have time to write a short letter, so I wrote a long one instead." (For more information on teaching summary writing, see Frey, Fisher, & Hernandez, 2003.)

Peter Eagan uses summary writing in his 5th grade science classroom to check his students' understanding. Weekly labs foster inquiry-based learning of science content. At the end of each lab, students write a précis describing what they did and what was observed. One lab focused on electrical circuits involved a battery, copper wiring, a lightbulb, and a lightbulb socket. When Mr. Eagan read his students' summaries, he realized that several students believed that the electricity only flowed when the lightbulb was touching the wire and that the wire was "empty" when the lightbulb was removed. The following day, Mr. Eagan engaged his students in a demonstration lesson using a length of garden hose. He allowed the hose to fill with water and then covered the end so that no water could come out. He asked students to decide whether the water was still in the hose. They all agreed that the water was still in the hose. He then explained that, like the water in the hose, the electricity remained in the wires even when the light bulb was not in the socket.

RAFT

Writing-to-learn prompts provide students with an opportunity to clarify their thinking and allow the teacher to peek inside their heads and check for understanding. Figure 4.5 lists a number of common writing-to-learn prompts. Our experience suggests that RAFT writing-to-learn prompts are especially helpful in checking for understanding.

RAFT writing prompts were designed to help students take different perspectives in their writing and thus their thinking (Santa & Havens, 1995). RAFT prompts provide a scaffold for students as they explore their writing based on various roles, audiences, formats, and topics (Fisher & Frey, 2004). RAFT prompts ask students to consider the following:

Role: What is the role of the writer?
Audience: To whom is the writer writing?
Format: What is the format for the writing?
Topic: What is the focus of the writing?

While RAFT prompts are typically used to teach perspective in writing, they can also be used to check for understanding. Teachers can design RAFT prompts based on all kinds of content, from lectures to films, readings, or labs. Using RAFT prompts as a tool to check for understanding requires that the teacher know what

Figure 4.5	Sample Writing-to-Learn Prompts

Admit Slips: Upon entering the classroom, students write on an assigned topic.
Examples: "Who was Gandhi and why should we care?"; "Describe the way sound waves travel."

Crystal Ball: Students describe what they think class will be about, what might happen next in the novel they're reading, or the next step in a science lab.

Found Poems: Students reread a piece of text, either something they have written or something published, and find key phrases. They arrange these into a poem structure without adding any new words.

Awards: Students recommend someone or something for an award that the teacher has created such as "Most helpful molecule" or "Most insidious leader."

Yesterday's News: Students summarize the information presented the day before in a film, lecture, discussion, or reading.

Take a Stand: Students discuss their opinions about a controversial topic.
Examples: "Is murder ever justified?"; "What's worth fighting for?"

Letters: Students write letters to others, including elected officials, family members, friends, or people who have made a difference.
Example: Students may respond to the prompt, "Write to Oppenheimer asking him to explain his position today."

Exit Slips: As a closure activity, students write on an assigned prompt.
Example: "The three best things I learned today are . . ."

Adapted from *Improving adolescent literacy: Strategies at work* (pp. 142–143), by D. Fisher and N. Frey, 2004, Upper Saddle River, NJ: Pearson/Merrill/Prentice Hall.

content learning he or she expects from students and that the prompt be constructed accordingly. For example, if a 3rd grade teacher wanted to know if students understood the life cycle of insects, he or she might use the following RAFT prompt:

R: Butterfly
A: Scientist
F: Journal entry
T: My experience with complete metamorphosis

A 6th grade social studies teacher who wanted to know if students understood the life and times of Marco Polo and the importance of the Silk Road might use the following RAFT prompt:

R: Marco Polo
A: Potential recruits

F: Recruitment poster

T: Come see the Silk Road!

And finally, a geometry teacher who wanted to know if students understood the characteristics of different types of triangles might use the following RAFT prompt:

R: Scalene triangle

A: Your angles

F: Text message

T: Our unequal relationship

RAFT prompts can also be used in conjunction with texts that students read. Fifth grade teacher Paul Johnson used a number of RAFT writing prompts during his unit on slavery. Mr. Johnson knows that students need to read widely, in books that they are able to and want to read, if they are to develop strong content knowledge (Ivey & Fisher, 2005). He selected a number of picture books on the topic of slavery for his students to read. To check for understanding, he wrote a RAFT prompt on the inside cover of each book. Examples of the RAFT prompts from this unit are included in Figure 4.6. A sample response written by April for one of the books can be found in Figure 4.7. Note the understanding of the complex issues surrounding slavery and the personal connections this student makes with the topic under study. Upon reading this response, Mr. Johnson knew that April was developing her understanding of the history content standard as well as an appreciation for human and civil rights.

Conclusion

Knowing that writing is thinking, that writing to learn clarifies students' thinking, and that writing allows teachers to check for understanding of content and ideas, wise teachers use any number of prompts to ensure their students learn. Of course, not all prompts are created equally. With some practice and experience, developing writing-to-learn prompts and tasks becomes easier and more fruitful. Some questions you might want to ask yourself as you create writing prompts to check for understanding include the following:

Figure 4.6	Sample RAFT Prompts

Minty: A Story of Young Harriet Tubman (Schroeder, 1996) **R** – Minty (Harriet Tubman) **A** – Old Ben **F** – Letter **T** – Thank you for everything you taught me	*Aunt Harriet's Underground Railroad in the Sky* (Ringgold, 1992) **R** – Cassie **A** – Bebe **F** – Invitation **T** – Let's go for a ride
Follow the Drinking Gourd (Winter, 1988) **R** – Conductor **A** – Passenger **F** – Song **T** – The path to freedom	*Sweet Clara and the Freedom Quilt* (Hopkinson, 1993) **R** – Conductor **A** – Traveler **F** – Message quilt **T** – A safe path through our town
The Underground Railroad (Stein, 1997) **R** – Dred Scott **A** – Chief Justice Roger Taney **F** – Court appeal **T** – Life as a slave in the United States	*Journey to Freedom: A Story of the Underground Railroad* (Wright, 1994) **R** – Joshua **A** – Slave catcher **F** – Response to the wanted ad **T** – My right to be free
From Slave Ship to Freedom Road (Lester, 1998) **R** – Author **A** – Reader **F** – Position statement **T** – Would you risk going to jail for someone you didn't know?	*A Picture Book of Harriet Tubman* (Adler, 1992) **R** – Slave catcher **A** – The public **F** – Wanted poster **T** – "Moses"

• Have you used explicit command words in your instructions (e.g., "compare and contrast" and "explain" are more explicit than "explore" or "consider")?

• Does the assignment suggest a topic, thesis, and format?

• Have you told students the kind of audience they are addressing—the level of knowledge they can assume the readers have and your particular preferences (e.g., "avoid slang"; "use the first-person sparingly")? (MIT Online Writing and Communication Center, 1999)

For more information on teaching writing as a discipline, see Frey and Fisher, 2006 and Fisher and Frey, 2007.

Figure 4.7	April's RAFT Response

January 1, 1865

Dear Old Ben,

I want to thank you for being my father and teaching me about freedom. You taught me to find the North Star in the sky and follow it to the north. You showed me how to read the moss on the trees. I could know my way. I could follow the north path to freedom.

I used everything I learned from you to help other people escape on my underground railroad. I couldn't have done it without your teaching me to find the north. Thank you for everything you taught me.

Your loving daughter,
Minty

5

Using Projects and Performances to Check for Understanding

Many of us recall participating in a classroom performance during our school years. It may have been a school play or a science fair. Perhaps you created a diorama in a shoebox illustrating the landing of the Pilgrims on Plymouth Rock. You may have constructed an animal cell out of Jell-O or built a model of a medieval castle. Whatever the project, it has undoubtedly lodged itself in your memories of school. Why are these activities so memorable? Because you were deeply invested in the outcome, you committed quite a bit of time and effort to the project or performance, and you recognized how different this was from the bulk of the assignments at which you toiled away every day.

The opportunity to apply learning to a novel situation hastens the transfer of learning. This concept is discussed often in educational courses but rarely realized in typical classroom settings. Although Bloom is well known for his work on a taxonomy of knowledge (see Chapter 3), what is sometimes overlooked is that one of the purposes of this system was to define ways in which a transfer of learning could occur. Tasks associated with application, analysis, synthesis, and evaluation are frequently designed as projects or performances. Many of these simply could not be accomplished by filling out a worksheet or answering multiple-choice questions. Ultimately, we must witness how our students choose and use information while taking part in a meaningful activity. When we view these events as opportunities to check for understanding and not just task completion, we gain insight into the extent to which our students have transferred their learning to new situations.

In addition to using oral language, questioning techniques, and writing, effective teachers incorporate projects and performances in their classrooms to determine students' understanding of the content. In this chapter, we focus on project- and problem-based learning and the outcomes from these initiatives in terms of documenting and analyzing student learning. Barron and colleagues (1998) refer to this kind of learning as "doing with understanding" (p. 271).

Misuses of Projects and Performances in the Classroom

To use projects and performances as a tool to determine students' understanding, it is necessary to move beyond the traditional view of culminating projects. These tasks should be seen as more than just a fun or rewarding payoff for having learned all that stuff. Nancy's high school experience of representing rough endoplasmic reticulum in animal cells with uncooked lasagna noodles in Jell-O was certainly fun and memorable. Unfortunately, this fun experience did not result in her ability to recall the purpose of the endoplasmic reticulum (it synthesizes proteins). Doug's experience in making tribal masks and baskets in his 3rd grade unit of study on local Native American populations resulted in a lot of papier-mâché art but not much understanding of the role that these items played in the daily life of the Kumeyaay. In these cases, it's likely that the "doing" part took precedence over the "understanding" part (Barron et al., 1998).

Home–school communication is essential when assigning and evaluating projects. We have seen models of California missions constructed by architect mothers and volcanoes with hydraulics installed by engineer fathers. Subsequent conversations with students reveal that they had little to do with the design or execution of the project, and as a result, they possess a limited understanding of the historical, mathematical, or scientific concepts the project was designed to foster. While we appreciate the efforts of well-meaning parents who stay up late to complete a project, it is important that they understand the intent of the assignment. After all, teachers are checking not for the parents' understanding of California history or earth science but the children's.

Design Principles for Projects and Performances

To maximize the potential of projects and performances to check for understanding, they must be carefully designed. Barron and colleagues (1998) describe four design principles necessary for learning to occur: "learning-appropriate goals, scaffolds for student and teacher learning, frequent opportunities for formative assessment and revision, and social organizations that promote participation" (p. 273).

Learning-Appropriate Goals

This first principle of design refers to the essential question you want your students to address. An essential question should cultivate a sense of curiosity and motivate students to seek answers. Essential questions should be open-ended and thought-provoking and not answerable with a simple yes or no (Wiggins & McTighe, 2005). For instance, Nancy may have better understood the functions of the organelles of an animal cell if the essential question had been "What are the common structures and functions of diverse organisms?" rather than "Can you build an animal cell from Jell-O?" Doug may have better understood the meaning of masks in Native American life if he had been furnished an essential question such as "How do humans celebrate?"

Scaffolds for Student and Teacher Learning

Most of us have learned that before engaging in a major project, it is wise to pilot a smaller version. In educational research, pilot surveys are administered to discover potential problems. Business organizations discuss "sending up a trial balloon" or "testing the waters" before launching an expensive endeavor. In similar fashion, Barron and colleagues (1998) advise providing students with a problem-based learning experience before assigning a major project. This primes students for potential difficulties and focuses their attention on the more pertinent conceptual aspects of the project. In addition, it scaffolds their understanding and provides useful feedback for the teacher, allowing misconceptions and poorly defined parameters to be addressed before too much time and effort have been invested. Moore and colleagues (1996) describe a study in which some students completed a problem-based case study simulation on writing business plans before executing one themselves.

The students who participated in the problem-based learning outperformed those who did not.

Frequent Opportunities for Formative Assessment and Revision

Projects and performances often demand a heavy investment of time and effort. Needless frustrations result when students have made that investment in good faith, only to discover that their end result misses the mark. More often than not, there were no systems in place to have work in progress assessed for revision.

We build incremental assessments into our project-based assignments to prevent these difficulties. For example, we assign a photo essay to our 9th grade writing class (Frey, 2003). This is quite an undertaking, and students' interest and enthusiasm run high. However, because we know the assignment is fraught with potential problems, we meet with each student several times over the course of the project. Students develop a storyboard, draft text, and assemble the final product. At each stage, we confer with them and complete a checklist (see Figure 5.1). In addition, we use a mutually constructed rubric at each stage so that they can gauge the level of completeness of their project (see Figure 5.2). These checklists and notes from our meetings are turned in with the final project. Of course, these tools can be modified for use with students with disabilities and for students who find school difficult.

Social Organizations That Promote Participation and a Sense of Agency

Many projects and performances involve group collaboration, and these instructional arrangements can be a source of frustration when not carefully designed and monitored. A common element in the findings about successful cooperative learning groups is that there should be both group and individual accountability (Cohen, 1994; Johnson & Johnson, 1998). Therefore, it is wise to provide students with a mechanism for evaluating their own performance in the group. We have included a sample self-assessment in Figure 5.3.

Projects that are completed individually may benefit from inviting peer feedback, which can be valuable for all students. Anyone engaged in a creative endeavor knows how useful it can be to run an idea past a trusted colleague.

Figure 5.1	Feedback for Draft Photo Essays

Feedback on Draft of Photo Essay

Student: _____ Date: _____ Draft # _____

CATEGORY	RESPONSIBILITIES
Conventions	☐ My paragraphs have more than one sentence. ☐ Each of my paragraphs has one main idea. ☐ I have used correct grammar. ☐ I have used correct punctuation. ☐ I have checked my spelling. ☐ I have used capital letters correctly. ☐ My handwriting is legible.
Organization	☐ My introduction is interesting and inviting. ☐ The sequence of ideas is logical. ☐ My ideas flow from one to another. ☐ I use helpful transitions between main points (e.g., "First of all" or "Similarly"). ☐ I have a satisfying conclusion.
Flow	☐ My sentences build logically upon the one(s) before. ☐ My sentences are different lengths. ☐ My sentences start in different ways. ☐ There are no run-on sentences. ☐ There are no incomplete sentences.
Punctuation	☐ Commas separate items in a series. ☐ A comma follows an introductory word or phrase. ☐ A semicolon connects two sentences. ☐ Closing quotation marks always follow commas or periods. ☐ Apostrophes are used correctly to show possession or to create contractions. ☐ A period, question mark, or exclamation point ends every sentence.
Word Choice	☐ I use descriptive words (adjectives and adverbs) often. ☐ I use strong, active verbs. ☐ I use synonyms and different words to add variety. ☐ My pronouns match the nouns to which they refer.

Next Steps:

From "A picture prompts a thousand words: Creating photo essays with struggling writers," by N. Frey, 2003, *California English, 8*(5), 20.

Figure 5.2	Rubric for Photo Essay

Student Name: _____   Date:_____   Title: _____

Category	4	3	2	1
Required Elements	Photo essay included all required elements as well as a few additional ones.	Photo essay included all required elements as well as one additional element.	Photo essay included all required elements.	One or more required elements were missing from the photo essay.
Spelling and Grammar	Few or no spelling or grammatical mistakes on a photo essay with lots of text.	Few or no spelling or grammatical mistakes on a photo essay with less text.	Several spelling or grammatical mistakes on a photo essay with lots of text.	Several spelling or grammatical mistakes on a photo essay with little text.
Use of Time	Used time well during each class period with no adult reminders.	Used time well during most class periods with no adult reminders.	Used time well but required adult reminders on one or more occasions.	Used time poorly in spite of several adult reminders.
Content	Photo essay uses both text and pictures to tell an imaginative story.	Photo essay uses mostly text, with some support from pictures, to tell an imaginative story.	Some pictures and text are not clearly related to one another.	Text and pictures have little connection with one another.

Required Elements:
- ☐ 15–20 photographs used in photo essay.
- ☐ Text is typed or written neatly.
- ☐ Photo essay includes a cover with title, author, and illustration.
- ☐ "About the Author" essay included.

From "A picture prompts a thousand words: Creating photo essays with struggling writers," by N. Frey, 2003, *California English, 8*(5), 21.

Peer response in the classroom can offer the same advantages, but the skills required for offering and accepting need to be taught. In particular, we remind our students of the following principles:

- • Students determine when they need peer feedback. We don't construct an artificial schedule of when students are required to get peer feedback, only that they do so at some point during the project.

Figure 5.3	Self-Assessment of Group Work

Name: _____

Date: _____

Project: _____

Members of my group:

_____

_____

_____

Please rank yourself based on your contributions to the group. Circle the number that best describes your work.

5 = Always   4 = Almost Always   3 = Sometimes   2 = Once or Twice   1 = Never

I completed my tasks on time.	5	4	3	2	1
I contributed ideas to the group.	5	4	3	2	1
I listened respectfully to the ideas of others.	5	4	3	2	1
I used other people's ideas in my work for the project.	5	4	3	2	1
When I was stuck, I sought help from my group.	5	4	3	2	1

Additional comments:

From *Language arts workshop: Purposeful reading and writing instruction* (p. 403), by N. Frey and D. Fisher, 2006, Upper Saddle River, NJ: Pearson/Merrill/Prentice Hall.

- Not everything needs peer feedback. Too much feedback can result in an overload of information.
- Teachers, not students, should offer feedback on the details and mechanics of the piece. Peer response should not turn classmates into miniature teachers. Instead, peers can provide reactions as a fellow reader, writer, or audience member related to what they understood and what might be confusing (Frey & Fisher, 2006).

Problem-Based and Project-Based Learning

Both problem-based and project-based learning (PBL) can be integrated into performances. These approaches seek to replicate an authentic experience or application that occurs outside the classroom. Most experiences are designed to be collaborative, resulting in social as well as academic learning. Both problem-based and project-based learning are intended to integrate skills and content across disciplines, resulting in a holistic experience.

Although the approaches are similar, there are some differences between the two. Project-based learning is more common to elementary and secondary classrooms; problem-based learning is used less frequently (Esch, 1998). Problem-based learning is used widely in the medical field, where case studies serve as an important method for developing the skills of novices (Hmelo, 1998). Because problem-based learning is, by design, authentic to the situation, young students are more limited in their ability to successfully complete these complex assignments. Therefore, project-based learning, where a multidimensional task is defined and supported, is used more frequently in K–12 classrooms.

Projects can extend from a few days in length to weeks or even a semester, with even young children finding success. For example, project-based learning has been used in inclusive 5th and 6th grade classrooms to teach historical understanding (Ferretti, MacArthur, & Okolo, 2001). While the potential of project-based learning is appealing, Meyer, Turner, and Spencer (1997) offer cautions regarding the design of such learning experiences. Having noted that some students have less capacity for dealing with setbacks and other challenges, they state that "typical classroom goals such as accuracy, speed, and completion dates may conflict with the project-based math goals of justification, thoughtfulness, and revision" (p. 517). Keep in mind some of the design principles discussed earlier, especially access to frequent formative assessments to guide revisions. These, along with structures such as timelines and intermediate goals, can be especially helpful for students who are less persistent or who like their work to be perfect before the teacher sees it.

Performance Learning

A third type of learning opportunity used frequently in the classroom is performance, which can be presented through public or other visual means. Many performances focus on the application and synthesis of knowledge to create novel products. Like project-based learning, there is an end product in mind (e.g., a poster, a Web-based project, a musical). Not all performances are as elaborate as problem- and project-based learning (PBL) assignments. Some are simpler and do not need all of the formal supports associated with PBL. For example, the creation of a graphic organizer to visually represent the influence of Muslim scholars on scientific processes, mathematics, and literature is not likely to require a series of formative assessments along the way.

The importance of performance opportunities lies in their potential for providing other outlets for students to demonstrate their mastery of different concepts in ways that are not limited to more traditional school-based demonstrations such as reading, writing, and computational tasks. In many ways, performance tasks lie at the heart of differentiated instruction because they afford learners with diverse needs creative ways to show competence (Tomlinson, 1999).

In the next section, we will discuss techniques for using performances and projects to check for understanding. All of them use principles of design discussed earlier, especially scaffolds and group interactions. Although many are public performances, some are transactions between the teacher and learner only.

Effective Techniques Using Projects and Performances

Readers' Theatre

Readers' Theatre is a classroom activity in which students read directly from scripts to tell a story or inform an audience. They do so without props, costumes, or sets. Readers' Theatre is first and foremost a *reading* activity, and students do not memorize their lines. They are, however, encouraged to use intonation, facial expression, prosody, and gestures appropriate to their characters and their characters' words. Readers' Theatre can be done with narrative or informational texts. The point is that students perform the reading.

Readers' Theatre enjoys a long history and a fairly strong research base. Readers' Theatre has been used to improve reading fluency, vocabulary knowledge, and comprehension (Doherty & Coggeshall, 2005; Flynn, 2004; Martinez, Roser, & Strecker, 1998–99). There are a number of ways that teachers can obtain Readers' Theatre scripts. The easiest way to find these is to type "readers' theatre scripts" into a Web search engine.

Using preproduced scripts will develop students' literacy skills, especially in the areas of fluency, vocabulary knowledge, and comprehension. However, preproduced scripts are not as useful in checking for understanding (unless you're evaluating fluency, for example). One way to use Readers' Theatre to check for understanding is to have small groups of students take a piece of text and turn it into a script. This allows the teacher to determine if the group (or individual students, for that matter) understands the main ideas of the texts. Alternatively, teachers can check students' understanding of specific content information using this method.

Sixth grade teacher Darleen Jackson uses Readers' Theatre to check for understanding of content. At one of the learning centers in her classroom, students create scripts from informational texts. The texts are selected based on the major units of study occurring at the time and represent a wide readability range. During their unit of study on ancient Egyptians, one group selected the book *Ancient Egypt* (Langley, 2005). They knew that they had to write their script, summarizing the main parts of the section they chose to read, and present the Readers' Theatre as a transition activity. Part of their performance is shown below:

Narrator: The earliest Egyptians lived in villages.

Egyptian Man 1: We decided to live in a small community.

Egyptian Man 2: It's safer when we live in a small community. Then we're not attacked by bandits or thieves.

Egyptian Man 1: We also can divide up the work. I'm a craftsman and make pottery.

Egyptian Man 2: I'm a trader who buys and sells things to keep our products moving along the Red Sea.

Egyptian Woman 1: There's no mention of what I'm doing for work, probably just taking care of the house and babies.

Narrator: Each small community developed their own leaders and religions.

When she listened to the group's Readers' Theatre presentation, Ms. Jackson knew that her students were developing an understanding of life in ancient Egypt. She was pleased that they questioned the role of women in ancient Egypt but wanted to be sure that they understood the development of commerce in this society. She planned to subsequently meet with this group and have them summarize their understandings to date.

Multimedia Presentations

Multimedia presentations provide learners an opportunity to share what they know as they combine text, graphics, video, sound, and even animation. Although such projects were unthinkable just a few years ago due to the costs of hardware and software involved, students today can produce complex products. The digital revolution has provided students with new ways of demonstrating their knowledge and has given teachers new ways of checking for understanding (Armstrong & Warlick, 2004). Research and practical evidence supporting the use of multimedia in the classroom are growing (Bremer & Bodley, 2004; Weiss, Kramarski, & Talis, 2006). There is evidence that multimedia projects facilitate student learning and provide students who are traditionally considered "at risk" with opportunities to demonstrate their knowledge (Garthwait, 2004; Maccini, Gagnon, & Hughes, 2002; Zydney, 2005).

Fourth grade teacher Michael Kluth spends much of the school year focused on the human body and its systems. Over the year, students develop and present several PowerPoint presentations. Mr. Kluth's students have to read widely about body systems they've selected in order to develop their understanding of the systems and to create their presentations. Mr. Kluth knows that these multimedia presentations allow him to check his students' understanding of the human body. He also knows that the projects enable his students to practice their listening and speaking skills. Groups present a body system each month and listen to at least 10 other presentations during that time (some of his students are in the library conducting their research while others are presenting). During these listening opportunities, students take Cornell notes (Frey & Fisher, 2007). This continual review of body systems and the cumulative knowledge students gain from developing their own multimedia presentations, as well as from listening to and taking notes on the presentations of others, allow Mr. Kluth the opportunity to evaluate his students in a meaningful way. As Mr. Kluth says, "The first set of presentations is just okay. They learn more for each system they complete and incorporate what they've learned from others. I can listen to the presentation and provide feedback on the content, common misconceptions, and their developing language skills."

Consistent with the appropriate use of a rubric, Mr. Kluth and his students review the criteria on which they are judged. Students should have an understanding of the multimedia project and performance rubric before they are given feedback. A sample rubric can be found in Figure 5.4.

Students in the Academy of Informational Technology, a school-within-a-school at Hoover High School in San Diego, created digital videos as a culminating project for several of their classes taught in an interdisciplinary format. The teachers chose to participate in the "My City Now" National Media Literacy Program (www. mycitynow.org). Students were assigned to make their own three-minute documentary about the past, present, or future of the city they live in. They were matched with senior citizens from the community to interview and were provided time in class and after school to work on their productions. The national winner for 2006 was Jonathan, a 14-year-old Hoover High School student who produced and directed a video titled *The Painting of a Culture*.

Jonathan's video highlighted Chicano Park in San Diego and its amazing murals. In fewer than three minutes, Jonathan documented the rise of a hardworking immigrant culture. According to his teachers, "Jonathan really demonstrated his understanding of the national immigration discussion. He did something with his understanding that will impact lots of people."

Electronic and Paper Portfolios

A portfolio is a collection of items intended to reflect a body of work. Architects and artists assemble professional portfolios to show clients their best work and to demonstrate their range of expertise. Educational portfolios differ slightly from those used by professionals in that they are designed to reflect a student's process of learning (Tierney, 1998). They are not meant to serve as a scrapbook of random ephemera gathered during the school year. At their best, they can provide another

Figure 5.4	Multimedia Project and Performance Rubric			
	4	3	2	1
Organization	Student presents information in a logical, interesting sequence that the audience can follow.	Student presents information in a logical sequence that the audience can follow.	Audience has difficulty following presentation because student does not consistently use a logical sequence.	Audience cannot understand presentation because there is no sequence of information.
Subject Knowledge	Student demonstrates full knowledge (more than required) by answering all class questions with explanations and elaboration.	Student is at ease and provides expected answers to all questions but fails to elaborate.	Student is uncomfortable with information and is able to answer only rudimentary questions.	Student does not have grasp of information; student cannot answer questions about subject.
Graphics	Student's graphics explain and reinforce screen text and presentation.	Student's graphics relate to text and presentation.	Student occasionally uses graphics that rarely support text and presentation.	Student uses superfluous graphics or no graphics.
Mechanics	Presentation has no misspellings or grammatical errors.	Presentation has no more than two misspellings and/or grammatical errors.	Presentation has three misspellings and/or grammatical errors.	Student's presentation has four or more spelling errors and/or grammatical errors.
Eye Contact	Student maintains eye contact with audience, seldom returning to notes.	Student maintains eye contact most of the time but frequently returns to notes.	Student occasionally uses eye contact but still reads most of report.	Student reads all of report with no eye contact.
Elocution	Student uses a clear voice and correct, precise pronunciation of terms so that all audience members can hear presentation.	Student's voice is clear. Student pronounces most words correctly. Most audience members can hear presentation.	Student's voice is low. Student incorrectly pronounces terms. Audience members have difficulty hearing presentation.	Student mumbles, incorrectly pronounces terms, and speaks too quietly for students in the back of class to hear.

From "Evaluating student presentations," by C. McCullen, 1997, Information Technology Evaluation Services, N.C. Department of Public Instruction. Retrieved February 7, 2007, from www.ncsu.edu/midlink/rub.pres.html.

way to check for understanding. However, this requires that the student choose the evidence that best illustrates his or her cognitive processes (Frey & Hiebert, 2003). An added benefit of portfolios is that they can involve parents in the process of checking their child's understanding (Flood & Lapp, 1989).

A challenge of portfolio creation is making decisions about what should be used. Wilcox (1997) proposes a model for portfolios that emphasizes the cognitive processes of learning, suggesting that the following items be included:

- Reading artifacts that make connections through reading, such as diagrams, outlines, and summaries.
- Thinking artifacts that construct our knowledge base, such as mind maps, steps to problem solving, and responses to prompts.
- Writing artifacts that make meaning through writing, such as self-evaluations, a publication piece, and reflections on a learning experience.
- Interacting artifacts that share and scaffold ideas, such as peer assessments, brainstorming charts, and a problem and solution.
- Demonstrating artifacts that show application and transfer of new learning, such as a project or exhibition. (p. 35)

Portfolios can be electronic or in a traditional paper-based format, usually stored in three-ring binders. Paper portfolios are generally easier for younger children to handle, as they can easily add new items and remove others with little assistance from an adult. Digital portfolios are increasingly used with older students, especially because this format has become essential to 21st-century classrooms. Experiences with the design and assembly of digital presentations also prepare students to create the electronic portfolios expected in higher education and the workplace.

Navigating the creation and maintenance of portfolios, whether paper or digital, with students can be tricky. Barrett (2006) tells the story of high school students who gathered after graduation to burn their portfolios. On the one hand, students need guidance in developing portfolios; on the other, the question of ownership in such a personal expression can be negatively affected by the required nature of many such assignments. The balance lies in teaching about types of artifacts, as suggested by Wilcox, and resisting formulaic approaches that require students to furnish three examples of this and four examples of that. The danger of such prescriptive portfolio assignments is that portfolios are reduced to filling in the blanks, thus reducing checking for understanding to task completion only.

Eighth grade teacher Tahira Birhanu taught her English class the basics of electronic portfolios at the beginning of the year so that students could choose to create them as a method for demonstrating their understanding of the works read and discussed in class. Her students know that a title card, table of contents, and buttons to activate links to sections of the portfolio are a must. Her primary interest is in analyzing the reflective and elaborative pieces the students include explaining the reading, writing, thinking, interacting, and demonstrating artifacts selected for the portfolio. One of the students in her class, Madison, chose to construct an electronic portfolio to explain her work with her literature circle, which had read *Project Mulberry* (Park, 2005). The story of a Korean American girl who rebels against being stereotyped as obedient and studious resonated with Madison, and she was eager to write about her thoughts. She included a collage comprising images captured from the Internet that represented the conflict the protagonist experienced. Madison also located links to Web sites that explained how silkworms are raised, since they become the focus of the science project discussed in the book. In addition to the collage and information, Madison included examples of notes she took during her reading and samples from the journal she kept for her literature circle group.

One of the reflective pieces that Madison wrote about regarding taking notes was included in her portfolio:

> When I heard we had to write notes as we read, all I could think of was, "Busy work!" I'm a good reader, and I don't need to be assigned reading to get into a good book. Taking notes was just going to slow me down. But when I reread some of my notes from earlier in the book, I could see how much my thinking had changed. I noticed that at the beginning of the book I thought that Julia was right to dislike anything that was "too Korean." My mom's always making me listen to all these old stories about people I hardly know. But when I read my notes for this project I started thinking about how maybe I wasn't being fair to my mom, just like Julia wasn't being fair to hers.

Ms. Birhanu was pleased to see how Madison had turned a reading artifact (her notes) into a demonstration of her transfer of learning.

Visual Displays of Information

In their book *Classroom Instruction That Works*, Marzano, Pickering, and Pollock (2001) describe visual displays (they call them "nonlinguistic representations") as "the most underused instructional strategy of all those reviewed" (p. 83). This is unfortunate, because the authors' meta-analysis of pertinent studies yielded a 0.75 effect size and a percentile gain of 28 on test scores. Visual displays of information require students to represent knowledge in a nonlinguistic fashion, typically using images or movement to do so. There is evidence that students who generate visual representations of a concept are better able to understand and recall the concept (Ritchie & Karge, 1996). Edens and Potter (2003) studied 184 4th and 5th graders who were learning about the law of conservation of energy. Those randomly assigned students who generated drawings scored higher on a test of conceptual knowledge and possessed fewer misconceptions than their peers who wrote in a science journal. They also noted in their study that the drawings themselves served as another means for assessing misconceptions and inaccuracies. It is likely that the use of visual representations of understanding assist the learner in building mental models (Mayer & Gallini, 1990). We discuss four types of visual representations below.

Graphic organizers. These are one of the most common and well-researched tools used in reading comprehension (Moore & Readence, 1984). Graphic organizers have been effectively used across the content areas, including in English and language arts (Egan, 1999), math (Monroe & Pendergrass, 1997), science (Carlson, 2000), and social studies (Landorf & Lowenstein, 2004). We know that graphic organizers are effective with students with disabilities (Dye, 2000; Kooy, 1992), students who are gifted and talented (Cassidy, 1989), English language learners (Levine, 1995) and across the grade spans of elementary school, middle school, high school, and college learners (Gonzalez, 1996; Hobbs, 2001; Williams et al., 2005).

While the instructional implications for graphic organizers are clear, the role that these visual representations play in assessment is less so. When teachers are checking for understanding, it seems reasonable to suggest that asking students to create a visual representation of their knowledge would be valuable. We're not suggesting that teachers learn to assess or evaluate the graphic organizers (e.g., how well the web is drawn) but rather that we use the construction of graphic organizers as a source of information to determine what students know and do not know.

As we have learned from the evidence on thinking maps (see, for example, www.thinkingmaps.com), students need to be taught to use a variety of visual tools and graphic organizers. We believe that this is necessary regardless of whether graphic organizers are used for instruction or to check for understanding. Simply photocopying a graphic organizer and requiring that students fill it out will not ensure deep learning or provide an authentic assessment opportunity (Egan, 1999; Frey & Fisher, 2007). Figure 5.5 contains a list of various types of graphic organizers and thinking maps with which students should be familiar.

Physics teacher Jesse Nunez uses graphic organizers in his class to check his students' understanding of content. He teaches his students a number of tools early in the school year and then invites them to use different tools to demonstrate their content knowledge. He does not provide photocopies of graphic organizers or require that students all use the same graphic organizer at the same time. During their unit of study on states of matter, Arian created a concept map explaining her knowledge of solids, liquids, and gases (see Figure 5.6). Mr. Nunez reviewed Arian's concept map and noted that she understood each of the three states of matter but wondered if she comprehended the interactions and relationships between and among these states of matter.

Inspiration. Like many things in our world, graphic organizers can also go digital. The Inspiration and Kidspiration software programs allow users to create visual tools—graphic organizers—on the screen (see www.inspiration.com for information). Current versions of the software allow users to import text, transform ideas and graphics, and select from a range of graphic organizers and tools.

Royer and Royer (2004) wondered if there was any difference in the complexity of the concept maps students would create if they had access to computers to complete the tasks. They compared the graphic organizers created by 52 students in biology classes that used either paper and pencil or computers with Inspiration software. Their findings suggest that there are significant positive outcomes when students create graphic organizers in a digital environment. Mastropieri, Scruggs, and Graetz (2003) document similar results and make similar recommendations for students who struggle with reading or who have disabilities.

Figure 5.5	Graphic Organizers and Definitions

primitives	Thinking Maps and the Frame	expanded maps

The Circle Map is used for seeking context. This tool enables students to generate relevant information about a topic as represented in the center of the circle. This map is often used for brainstorming.

The Bubble Map is designed for the process of describing attributes. This map is used to identify character traits (language arts), cultural traits (social studies), properties (sciences), or attributes (mathematics).

The Double Bubble Map is used for comparing and contrasting two things, such as characters in a story, two historical figures, or two social systems. It is also used for prioritizing which information is most important within a comparison.

The Tree Map enables students to do both inductive and deductive classification. Students learn to create general concepts, (main) ideas, or category headings at the top of the tree, and supporting ideas and specific details in the branches below.

The Brace Map is used for identifying the part-whole, physical relationships of an object. By representing whole–part and part–subpart relationships, this map supports students' spatial reasoning and understanding of how to determine physical boundaries.

The Flow Map is based on the use of flowcharts. It is used by students for showing sequences, order, timelines, cycles, actions, steps, and directions. This map also focuses students on seeing the relationships between stages and substages of events.

The Multi-Flow Map is a tool for seeking causes of events and the effects. The map expands when showing historical causes and for predicting future events and outcomes. In its most complex form, it expands to show the interrelationships of feedback effects in a dynamic system.

The Bridge Map provides a visual pathway for creating and interpreting analogies. Beyond the use of this map for solving analogies on standardized tests, this map is used for developing analogical reasoning and metaphorical concepts for deeper content learning.

The Frame
The "metacognitive" Frame is not one of the eight Thinking Maps. It may be drawn around any of the maps at any time as a "meta-tool" for identifying and sharing one's frame of reference for the information found within one of the Thinking Maps. These frames include personal histories, culture, belief systems, and influences such as peer groups and the media.

Figure 5.6	Arian's Concept Map

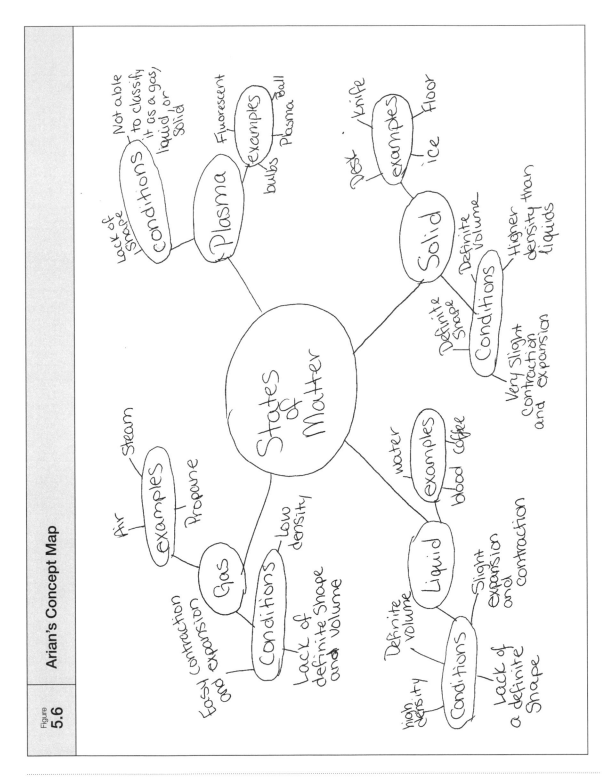

During their study of insects, complete and incomplete metamorphosis, and life cycles, the students in Jenny Olson's class spent time at a learning center creating visual representations of their understanding using Inspiration. Javier created the visual representation—a concept map—of complete metamorphosis found in Figure 5.7. Ms. Olson noticed that Javier had an understanding of the stages of complete metamorphosis and had collected some interesting details about each stage from the various books he had read. However, she also noted that his visual representation did not communicate the stage and cycle information critical to understanding the process of metamorphosis and the insect life cycle. She decided to meet with him and discuss his graphic organizer. Through questioning, she led Javier to understand how to represent his learning visually. She also had the opportunity to solidify his understanding that eggs become larvae, larvae become pupae, pupae become adults, and then the adults lay eggs.

Foldables. Foldables are three-dimensional interactive graphic organizers developed by Zike (1992). They provide students with a way of manipulating concepts and information in ways that are far more kinesthetic than ordinary worksheets. Paper is folded into simple shapes that reflect the conceptual relationships represented by the notes. Sixth grade social studies teacher Tim Valdes asked students to compare and contrast the Athenians and Spartans of ancient Greece. His students had been working with interactive graphic organizers since the beginning of the school year, so they were able to select their own way of representing this information. Arturo chose to make a three-tab book with a Venn diagram drawn on the front. Under each flap, he wrote information about both city-states. Arturo's choice of an organizer and the information he included gave Mr. Valdes insight into the knowledge his student possessed, as well as the mental model he used. Arturo's Foldable is represented in Figure 5.8.

Dioramas. Though some believe dioramas are old-fashioned, we are proponents of dioramas as a method of performance. Unlike the dioramas of our youth, which tended to emphasize the composition of the final product over the learning invested in its development, the potential of a diorama is akin to any other visual representation of knowledge. Dioramas are miniature models of a scene from the physical, social, biological, or narrative world, traditionally built inside a shoebox turned on its side. We prefer to use the Foldables four-door diorama shown in Figure 5.9

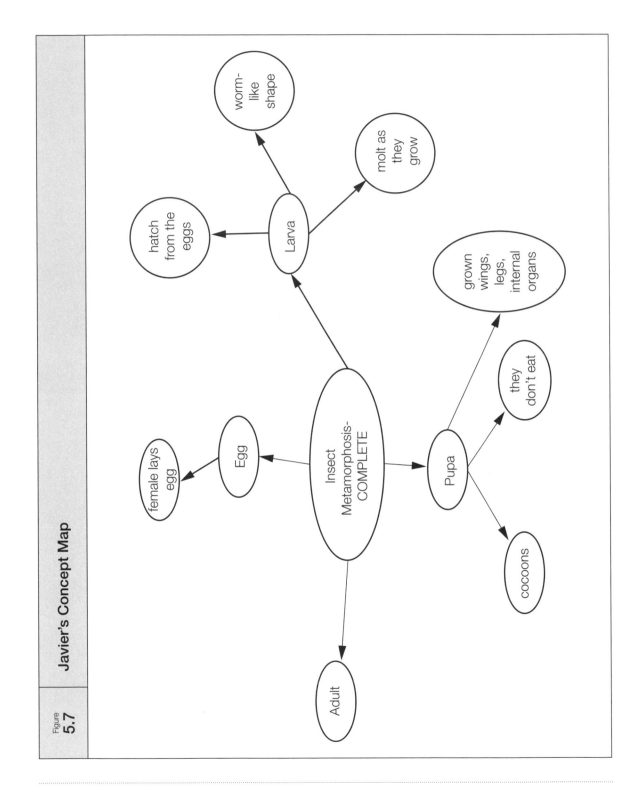

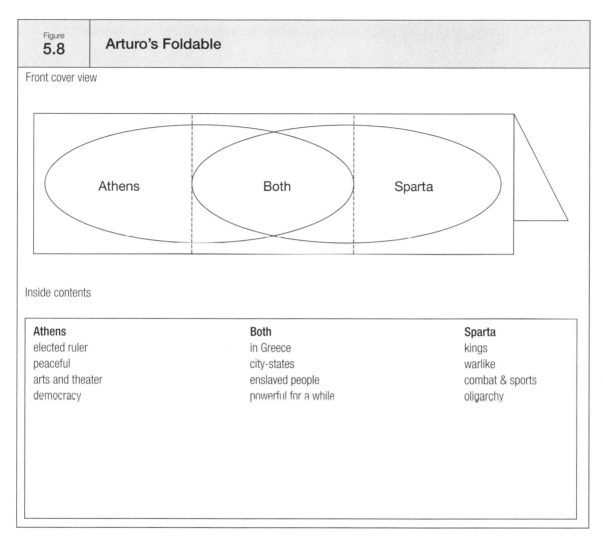

Figure 5.8 — Arturo's Foldable

Front cover view

Athens Both Sparta

Inside contents

Athens	Both	Sparta
elected ruler	in Greece	kings
peaceful	city-states	warlike
arts and theater	enslaved people	combat & sports
democracy	powerful for a while	oligarchy

because it offers the student more options in the size of the diorama (they can use anything from 11" × 17" paper up to poster board size).

Louis Daguerre, the inventor of the daguerreotype, was the first to conceive the use of dioramas. He was a set designer by trade, and he developed large-scale dioramas (more than 20 feet in length) for public display, their subject usually an architectural wonder (Maggi, 1999). Using a *chiaroscuro* painting technique (i.e., the arrangement or treatment of light and dark parts in a pictorial work of art) and lighting methods learned in the theater, Daguerre introduced the world to a unique style of visual storytelling.

Figure 5.9	Four-Door Diorama

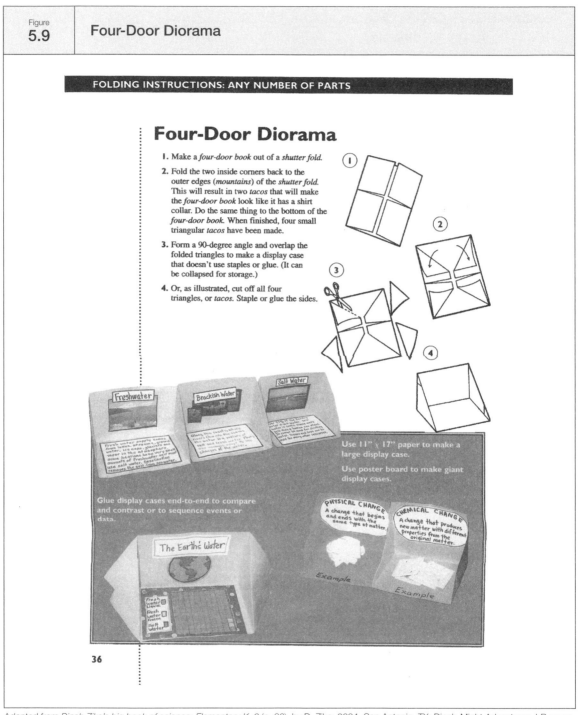

FOLDING INSTRUCTIONS: ANY NUMBER OF PARTS

Four-Door Diorama

1. Make a *four-door book* out of a *shutter fold*.

2. Fold the two inside corners back to the outer edges (*mountains*) of the *shutter fold*. This will result in two *tacos* that will make the *four-door book* look like it has a shirt collar. Do the same thing to the bottom of the *four-door book*. When finished, four small triangular *tacos* have been made.

3. Form a 90-degree angle and overlap the folded triangles to make a display case that doesn't use staples or glue. (It can be collapsed for storage.)

4. Or, as illustrated, cut off all four triangles, or *tacos*. Staple or glue the sides.

Use 11" x 17" paper to make a large display case.

Use poster board to make giant display cases.

Glue display cases end-to-end to compare and contrast or to sequence events or data.

36

Adapted from *Dinah Zike's big book of science: Elementary K–6* (p. 36), by D. Zike, 2004, San Antonio, TX: Dinah-Might Adventures, LP, www.dinah.com.

It is this visual narrative that offers a way of checking for understanding. By examining the information represented in the diorama, as well as talking with students about how they represented the information, you can check for their understanding of the concepts. Third grade teacher Belinda Mullins uses dioramas as a way for students to demonstrate what they have learned about animals they have researched in science. Emily chose to learn about the Mexican free-tailed bat. She constructed a diorama that included a drawing of a small brown bat flying out of a cave. Emily hung the bat drawing from a piece of yarn attached to the top of the diorama to represent flight, and she lined the inside of the box with black construction paper. She glued small "googly eyes" purchased from a craft store at the opening of the cave. Tiny drops of brown puff paint dotted the inside of the display. She explained to Ms. Mullins that this bat lives in caves and flies at night. Some caves are filled with millions of Mexican free-tailed bats, making them some of the largest colonies on Earth (that's what the "googly eyes" were for). Ms. Mullins told Emily that she understood that the black construction paper represented the night sky, but what were the brown dots of paint meant to be? Emily replied, "Those are the mosquitoes they eat every night!" By making sure that she met with Emily and each of her students, Ms. Mullins was able to check their understanding about the animals they had selected as the subject for their first science research project.

Public Performances

The act of performing publicly can be a memorable experience for students and teachers. As noted earlier in this chapter, public performances can also be used as a means for checking for understanding. McDonald (2005) has written of the value of student-created performances to gauge the learning of students in art; McDonald and Fisher (2002) addressed the same subject in music education. Podlozny's (2000) meta-analysis indicates that when students received instruction on public performance, there was an increase in comprehension and, to a lesser extent, reading achievement. In recent years, many high schools have begun to require public exhibitions of knowledge as part of the graduation requirements for seniors.

Rita Elwardi and Sheri Sevenbergen's students in their high school ESL classes engage in an extended public performance of their learning in an exhibition that has come to be known as "The Quilt Celebration." Their students come from every continent except Antarctica and Australia, and together they represent the range of human experiences associated with immigration to America. Over the course of the year, students construct a quilt made of individual squares that visually represent their stories. They write poetry collaboratively for public performance at the celebration. Students discuss their transformation through learning and their plans to continue their education. The celebration is attended by a large audience of families, faculty, students, and community members. As you can imagine, the event is moving; audience members are sometimes brought to tears as they listen to the insightful comments of these adolescents. However, Ms. Elwardi and Ms. Sevenbergen also use these public performances as a way to check for understanding. As Ms. Elwardi notes, "They need to be able to tell their own stories, and to relate who they are and what they stand for to others. As new arrivals to this country, it's easy for them to become intimidated by the language. This event gives them an opportunity to tell their story more formally, which is practice for a lifetime of effective communication." The students wrote and performed several poems for the Quilt Celebration in 2006, one of which can be found in Figure 5.10.

Figure 5.10	Poem from the Quilt Celebration
	I used to be a grain of sand, caught in an oyster shell, but now I am a pearl, reflecting the luminous moon of possible dreams. I used to be a closed fist, clenched in anger, but now I am an open hand, extending friendship. I used to be a caterpillar, always stuck on a leaf, but now I am a butterfly— flying for freedom and looking for love. I used to be the starless night, hiding my dreams in darkness,

but now I am a prism of light
illuminating my way into the future.

I used to be a hard lump of coal
under the ground,
but now I am a glittering diamond,
valuable and precious.

I used to be a blank piece of paper,
but now I am a journal full of ideas.

I used to be a moon,
sometimes full, sometimes half,
sometimes just a sliver of myself,
but now I am a star sending light
to unknown worlds.

I used to be a paper crane,
folded to resemble something real,
but now my wings take me
to the height of my hopes and dreams.

I used to be lead, held by a pencil,
but now I am the words,
bringing ideas to life on paper.

I used to be a seed,
fallen to the ground,
but now I am a giant tree
with branches that give others shade.

Conclusion

Projects and performances are an underused but critical method of checking for understanding. These displays offer students an opportunity to use new learning to create original works, allowing a transfer of learning to occur. By using the design principles put forth by Barron and colleagues (1998), teachers can ensure that more meaningful work is generated. While some tasks require extensive preparation for their execution, such as portfolios and public performances, many others, such as visual displays of information and Readers' Theatre, are easily integrated into daily classroom practice.

6

Using Tests to Check for Understanding

In this era of accountability, student understanding is ultimately measured by tests. In this chapter, we explore the use of tests to determine what students know and don't know. We discuss the schools that are beating the odds by providing students with test format practice throughout the year and teaching students about tests as a genre (similar to biographies or science fiction). We also provide guidelines for creating a variety of constructed-response test items, including multiple choice, short answer, dichotomous choices, and essays.

We recognize the anxiety that tests can provoke in students. This anxiety is heightened for those who feel unprepared, unskilled, or psychologically uneasy. We have both witnessed our share of students who have become emotionally distraught and even physically ill at the sight of a test. Empathy for our students should be balanced with hard questions about our role in their apprehension. If tests are really intended to check for understanding, we need our students to perform at their optimal level. What factors are contributing to their mental state? Have we adequately prepared them for the content being tested? Have we taught them to be "test-wise"? Can we recognize the difference in student performance results when either factor is problematic?

We believe that information is power and when teachers understand the purposes and limitations of various tests and approaches, their students will profit.

However, our students cannot fully benefit if we do not take the time to explain how tests work. Even more importantly, we need to help our students understand the purposes for testing. Far too many students believe that their futures ride on the outcome of a single test. Sadly, that is sometimes true. We are appalled at reports of informal reading inventories being misused to make in-grade retention decisions for 1st graders. We worry about high school students who decide to drop out of school because their performance on the state exit exam has confirmed in their minds that they are not smart enough to succeed academically. And we are depressed when a student raises his or her hand in the middle of an engaging lesson to ask, "Is this going to be on the test?"

While we cannot single-handedly change the testing climate overnight, we can create classrooms where testing is understood and appreciated by teachers and students for what it can accomplish. There are two implications for this proposal. The first is that we must understand what different tests do and share that information with our students. The second is that we must develop a classroom climate that empowers students in their quest to check their own understanding. In other words, testing should not have the sole purpose of extracting a grade. It can be a method for learners to monitor their own understanding and to act upon their own learning. When students are encouraged to set goals, and tests are linked to those goals, learners can be motivated to actively engage in their own learning (Tuckman, 1998). Keep in mind, too, that if you are checking for understanding in the many ways discussed in this book, the need for a single test to evaluate student performance is eliminated. Furthermore, students of teachers who are continually checking for understanding benefit from assessment and feedback across their learning day.

Why Use Tests?

Tests and assessments are used for a variety of purposes. Lapp, Fisher, Flood, and Cabello (2001) identify the following four reasons tests and assessments are commonly used:

- Diagnosing individual student needs (e.g., assessing developmental status, monitoring and communicating student progress, certifying competency, determining needs);

- Informing instruction (e.g., evaluating instruction, modifying instructional strategies, identifying instructional needs);
- Evaluating programs; or
- Providing accountability information. (p. 7)

Given these diverse uses of tests and assessments, it seems reasonable to suggest that there are, or have been, misuses of this technique. As a principal friend of ours says, "You can't fatten the cattle just by weighing 'em." We agree. You have to *do* something with the information you get from tests and assessments. It's important to remember that there are good and appropriate uses of tests. In checking for understanding, tests are used for the second purpose noted above—to inform instruction. Before we continue with our discussion on the appropriate uses of tests and assessments, let's consider their potential misuses.

Misuses of Tests in the Classroom

Consider the history of educational testing. Tests of one kind or another have been around for a long time (Webb, 2006). But the world changed with the advent of the IQ test (Gould, 1981). The IQ test brought science, the scientific process, and "hard data" to education. At this point in history, most fields and professions were being influenced by the successes in manufacturing, Progressive Era thinking in general, and the focus on the efficiency movement in particular (Gould, 2001). In essence, the dominant idea of the time was that the scientific study of a problem would lead to answers and an unambiguous solution. Professionals, such as physicians, looked for specific tools they could use in studying and solving issues.

The IQ test appeared to be the scientific tool that would work for education. It allowed educators to function as professionals or experts with a set of tools at their disposal. Educators could "scientifically" evaluate a child's ability—their intelligence quotient, as Terman (1916) labeled it. Using the IQ test, educators believed that they could determine the future success of a child and track the child into appropriately demanding classes based on his or her ability. To educators of the day living in the Progressive Era, this seemed both scientific and child focused; it wouldn't burden the "mentally deficient" (in the vocabulary of the time), nor would it prevent gifted and talented students from accessing more challenging work. The labeling system based on IQ tests used during this period of time can be found in

Figure 6.1. While it is hard to imagine using these terms and labels today, it does cause us to question the labels we use for students based on the assessments and tests available to us today.

Figure 6.1	Classification Based on IQ Test Results	
IQ Range	**Classification**
140 and over	Genius or near genius
120–140	Very superior intelligence
110–120	Superior intelligence
90–110	Normal or average intelligence
80–90	Dullness
70–80	Borderline deficiency
50–69	Moron
20–49	Imbecile
Below 20	Idiot

Over the next several decades, educators debated the usefulness of the IQ test and searched for more valid, reliable, and culturally sensitive measures of children's intellectual ability. In the 1960s and 1970s, IQ tests began to fall out of favor, partially because of racially and culturally specific test questions and partially because they did not deliver on their promise. In 1964, the New York City Board of Education eliminated IQ testing entirely. In 1983, Howard Gardner argued that reason, intelligence, logic, and knowledge are not synonymous; introduced the world to a theory of multiple intelligences; and reaffirmed Binet's belief that intelligence was complex and could not be easily measured by a single score.

The current focus on testing is the latest cycle of the on-again, off-again use of tests in public schooling. And it should come as no surprise that there are critics (and concerned individuals) of this high-accountability phase of education (see, for example, Graves, 2002; Kohn, 2000; Popham, 2003). Critics typically cluster their concerns about standardized testing into the following four areas (Yeh, 2005):

- Narrowing the curriculum by excluding subject matter not tested. For example, with a significant focus on reading and math, the concern is that social studies, music, and art are being neglected because they are not commonly tested.
- Excluding topics either not tested or not likely to appear on the test even within tested subjects. For example, oral language (i.e., speaking and listening) is not commonly tested as part of the language arts and is therefore at risk in the classroom.
- Reducing learning to the memorization of easily recalled facts for multiple-choice testing. For example, students are taught to memorize math formulas rather than understand how and when to use such formulas.
- Devoting too much classroom time to test preparation rather than learning. For example, spending the first 10 minutes of each period focused on sample test questions rather than the content students need to know in order to master the subject or discipline.

Interestingly, in her study comparing higher- and lower-performing schools, Langer (2001) found that teachers in the higher-performing schools use tests as an opportunity to "revise and reformulate their curriculum" (p. 860). She reports, "While they do practice format before a test, not much teaching time is devoted to it. Rather, infusion is the key" (p. 861). Langer finds a direct contrast in lower-performing schools. There, teachers "treated tests as an additional hurdle, separated from their literacy curriculum. In these schools the test-taking focus seems to be on teaching to the test-taking skills rather than gaining skills and knowledge" (p. 862). This application of testing is not the only thing that teachers in higher-performing schools do differently; they also infuse literacy skills into and across the curriculum.

This is similar to the work done by Fullan, Hill, and Crévola (2006), who note that an educational "breakthrough" is possible. In their words,

> The key to this transformation lies in the smart use of data to drive instruction. Currently, many school systems collect data and feed it back to districts and schools. Much of this feedback is rudimentary and surface level. Where deeper feedback occurs, teachers are not helped to know what to do with it. Even if the data are better analyzed, teachers do not know how to

translate the information into powerful, focused instruction that responds to individual students' needs. (p. xvi)

We agree with Fullan and his colleagues and the findings from the Langer study. In our experience, it is through checking for understanding that students learn to demonstrate their knowledge in a variety of ways (including on tests) and that teachers can make needed curricular changes and implement instructional innovations. While we are focused on checking for understanding using formative rather than summative assessments (such as standardized state tests), we do know that regular practice, feedback, and focused instruction based on individual student needs will change learning outcomes (Fisher, 2005; Fisher, Lapp, & Flood, 2005). Let's consider a number of ways to design tests that can provide teachers with opportunities to check for understanding.

Using Tests to Check for Understanding

Checking for understanding using tests is dependent in part on the design and development of good test items. Figure 6.2 provides a checklist useful in the development of different types of testing items. However, checking for understanding using tests is equally dependent on the analysis of student responses. Of course, this is not unique to tests. All of the systems for checking for understanding we have discussed in this book require an analysis of student responses as well as instructional decisions based on those individual responses.

Multiple Choice

Multiple-choice items are probably the most common type of objective test question (Linn & Miller, 2005). They provide the teacher with an opportunity to gauge students' understanding in a fairly quick and efficient manner. They also are easy to analyze in that incorrect responses can be clustered as percentages and teachers can easily determine which of the incorrect responses students most commonly selected. A list of the advantages and disadvantages of multiple-choice items can be found in Figure 6.3.

Figure 6.2	**Checklist for Creating Common Assessments**

All Items

☐ Is this the most appropriate type of item to use for the intended learning outcomes?

☐ Does each item or task require students to demonstrate the performance described in the specific learning outcome it measures (relevance)?

☐ Does each item present a clear and definite task to be performed (clarity)?

☐ Is each item or task presented in simple, readable language and free from excessive verbiage (conciseness)?

☐ Does each item provide an appropriate challenge (ideal difficulty)?

☐ Does each item have an answer that would be agreed upon by experts (correctness)?

☐ Is there a clear basis for awarding partial credit on items or tasks with multiple points (scoring rubric)?

☐ Is each item or task free from technical errors and irrelevant clues (technical soundness)?

☐ Is each test item free from cultural bias?

☐ Have the items been set aside for a time before reviewing them (or having them reviewed by a colleague)?

Short-Answer Items

☐ Can the items be answered with a number, symbol, word, or brief phrase?

☐ Has textbook language been avoided?

☐ Have the items been stated so that only one response is correct?

☐ Are the answer blanks equal in length (for fill-in responses)?

☐ Are the answer blanks (preferably one per item) at the end of the items, preferably after a question?

☐ Are the items free of clues (such as *a* or *an*)?

☐ Has the degree of precision been indicated for numerical answers?

☐ Have the units been indicated when numerical answers are expressed in units?

Binary (True–False) and Multiple-Binary Items

☐ Can each statement be clearly judged true or false with only one concept per statement?

☐ Have specific determiners (e.g., usually, always) been avoided?

☐ Have trivial statements been avoided?

☐ Have negative statements (especially double negatives) been avoided?

☐ Does a superficial analysis suggest a wrong answer?

☐ Are opinion statements attributed to some source?

☐ Are the true and false items approximately equal in length?

☐ Is there approximately an equal number of true and false items?

☐ Has a detectable pattern of answers (e.g., T, F, T, F) been avoided?

Matching Items

☐ Is the material for the two lists homogeneous?

☐ Is the list of responses longer or shorter than the list of premises?

☐ Are the responses brief and on the right-hand side?

☐ Have the responses been placed in alphabetical or numerical order?

☐ Do the directions indicate the basis for matching?

☐ Do the directions indicate how many times each response may be used?

☐ Are all of the matching items on the same page?

Figure 6.2	**Checklist for Creating Common Assessments** (*continued*)

Multiple-Choice Items

☐ Does each item stem present a meaningful problem?
☐ Is there too much information in the stem?
☐ Are the item stems free of irrelevant material?
☐ Are the item stems stated in positive terms (if possible)?
☐ If used, has negative wording been given special emphasis (e.g., capitalized)?
☐ Are the distractors brief and free of unnecessary words?
☐ Are the distractors similar in length and form to the answer?
☐ Is there only one correct or clearly best answer?
☐ Are the distractors based on specific misconceptions?
☐ Are the items free of clues that point to the answer?
☐ Are the distractors and answer presented in sensible (e.g., alphabetical, numerical) order?
☐ Has "all of the above" been avoided and has "none of the above" been used judiciously?
☐ If a stimulus is used, is it necessary for answering the item?
☐ If a stimulus is used, does it require use of skills sought to be assessed?

Essay Items

☐ Are the questions designed to measure higher-level learning outcomes?
☐ Does each question clearly indicate the response expected (including extensiveness)?
☐ Are students aware of the basis on which their answers will be evaluated?
☐ Are appropriate time limits provided for responding to the questions?
☐ Are students aware of the time limits and/or point values for each question?
☐ Are all students required to respond to the same questions?

Performance Items

☐ Does the item focus on learning outcomes that require complex cognitive skills and student performances?
☐ Does the task represent both the content and skills that are central to learning outcomes?
☐ Does the item minimize dependence on skills that are irrelevant to the intended purpose of the assessment task?
☐ Does the task provide the necessary scaffolding for students to be able to understand the task and achieve the task?
☐ Do the directions clearly describe the task?
☐ Are students aware of the basis (expectations) on which their performances will be evaluated in terms of scoring rubrics?

For the Assessment as a Whole

☐ Are the items of the same type grouped together on the test (or within sections, sets)?
☐ Are the items arranged from easy to more difficult within sections or the test as a whole?
☐ Are items numbered in sequence, indicating so if the test continues on subsequent pages?
☐ Are all answer spaces clearly indicated and is each answer space related to its corresponding item?
☐ Are the correct answers distributed in such a way that there is no detectable pattern?
☐ Is the test material well spaced, legible, and free of typos?
☐ Are there directions for each section of the test and the test as a whole?
☐ Are the directions clear and concise?

Adapted from *Measurement and assessment in teaching* (9th ed.), by R. L. Linn and M. D. Miller, 2005, Upper Saddle River, NJ: Merrill Prentice Hall.

Figure 6.3	Advantages and Disadvantages of Multiple-Choice Items	
Advantages		**Disadvantages**
Allows for assessment of a wide range of learning objectives, from factual to evaluative understanding		Quality items are difficult and time-consuming to develop
Analyzing patterns of incorrect responses may provide diagnostic information		Tendency for items to focus on low-level learning objectives
Permits wide sampling and broad coverage of content domain due to students' ability to respond to many items		Assessment results may be biased by students' reading ability and test savvy
Allows the comparison and evaluation of related ideas, concepts, or theories		May overestimate learning due to the ability to utilize an elimination process for answer selection
Permits manipulation of difficulty level by adjusting the degree of similarity among response options		Does not measure the ability to organize and express ideas
Amenable to item analysis		Generally does not provide effective feedback to correct errors in understanding
Objective nature limits bias in scoring		
Easily administered to large numbers of students		
Efficient to score either manually or via automatic means		
Limits assessment bias caused by poor writing skills		
Less influenced by guessing than true–false items		

Adapted from *Effective multiple-choice items,* by B. J. Mandernach, 2003c. Retrieved July 7, 2006, from www.park.edu/cetl/quicktips/multiple. html

Multiple-choice items consist of two parts: a stem and a number of response options. In other words, the multiple-choice item presents a problem and a list of possible solutions. Both of these parts are important to the creation of a good test item.

The stem. The stem establishes a problem in the mind of the test taker. Therefore, it is important that the stem itself is not ambiguous, resulting in a test taker needlessly led astray by semantics. Consider the two stems in Figure 6.4. You'll see that the stem significantly influences students' understanding of the task at hand.

We were reminded of this while proctoring a middle school math exam. Luis, an English language learner classified as a "beginner," read the instructions that said, "Find x." He raised his hand to get our attention. He pointed to his paper where the letter x was circled and asked, "Like this?"

Stems may be written as either direct questions or incomplete statements. An example of a direct question format looks like this:

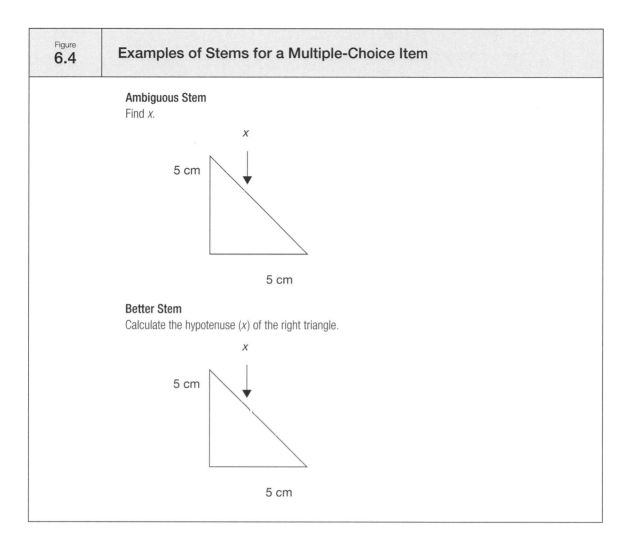

Figure 6.4 — Examples of Stems for a Multiple-Choice Item

Ambiguous Stem
Find *x*.

Better Stem
Calculate the hypotenuse (*x*) of the right triangle.

Which of the following insects has a pupa stage in its metamorphosis?

The incomplete statement form would read:

An example of an insect that has a pupa stage is _____ .

The response options. Obviously, the first rule to a good multiple-choice question is that only one answer can be correct. This doesn't mean that *all of the above* and *none of the above* cannot be used as a response option. However, it is critical that each response option is scrupulously evaluated for accuracy. Be certain to pay attention to the grammatical structures of the response options, as errors in syntax can confuse students and result in incorrect answers that are the product of poor construction, rather than a lack of understanding.

Distractors are more difficult to write than the correct answer, and it is not uncommon to see poorly constructed multiple-choice questions that contain at least one response option that is simply preposterous. This is a lost opportunity, as well as an indication that the person who constructed the test does not have an understanding of what students know and do not know. The best distractors address misconceptions, oversimplifications, and overgeneralizations that students may possess about the topic. This is different from a simple wrong answer, which is likely to be recognized by most students as coming from left field. When distractors are developed with misconceptions in mind, teachers and students can pinpoint what is understood and not understood. They become diagnostic distractors and allow for teaching with precision (see Chapter 7 for more information on using diagnostic distractors to make teaching decisions). Consider the example in Figure 6.5.

Figure 6.5	**Multiple-Choice Item with Distractors**	
Stem: A plant is able to grow larger because		
A. it gets its food from the soil.	Misconception	A student who chooses this answer does not understand that nutrients are manufactured internally by the plant.
B. it turns water and air into sugar.	Oversimplification	The student understands that food is manufactured internally but does not understand that water and carbon dioxide (from the air) are used to make sugar and oxygen.
C. it has chlorophyll to produce food.	Overgeneralization	The student does not understand that some parasitic plants do not contain chlorophyll.
D. it adds biomass through photosynthesis.	Correct answer	

Selection of any one of the incorrect answers (A, B, or C) yields information about what the student does not know as well as what he or she does know. Additionally, none of the choices is so far askew that it serves no purpose other than to increase the probability that a test taker can guess correctly. Notice that the example does not unnecessarily give away the correct answer by using absolutes like "never" and "always" (test-wise students know these are usually incorrect). Savvy students also anticipate that correct answers are significantly shorter or longer than the distractors. If you use a noticeably shorter or longer response option, consider making it a distractor.

A great resource for test creation, regardless of the format, is www.easytestmaker.com. This Web site allows you to enter the test items and will format it for you. There are services on the Web site that cost a nominal fee, but the test maker program is free.

Short Answer

Short-answer and completion items are both forms of "supply" items in which students have to provide the response, rather than selecting one from a teacher-generated list (as in a multiple-choice item). Short-answer test items (also called completion, supplied-response, or constructed-response items) are those that can be answered by a word, phrase, number, or symbol (Linn & Miller, 2005). They are generally considered effective as a measure of students' ability to accurately recall specific information. Short-answer items require that students either complete a statement (fill-in-the-blank or completion items) or answer a direct question using a single word or brief phrase. The advantages and disadvantages of short-answer items are presented in Figure 6.6.

Instructional objectives that require students to know certain information (e.g., those that suggest that the student recall, label, name, list, state, define, or describe) can be measured with short-answer or completion items. There are a number of common formats for these supply-type items; teachers must consider the following issues when making a decision about which format to use.

The blank line. One decision required for the use of short-answer or completion items concerns the blank line. Does the student write on the line or in another designated place? (Remember, the directions about this should be clear). In the first example below, the student writes his or her response on the blank line at the end of the sentence. In the second example below, the student writes his or her response on the blank line to the right of the sentence:

Hydrogen has an atomic number of _____.
Hydrogen has an atomic number of _____. _____

Figure 6.6	Advantages and Disadvantages of Short-Answer Items	
Advantages		**Disadvantages**
Scores less likely to be influenced by guessing		Accuracy of assessment may be influenced by handwriting/ spelling skills
Requires increased cognitive ability to generate answers		Subjective nature can make scoring difficult and time-consuming
Provides diagnostic information when looking at types of errors		Difficult to write items so that desired knowledge is clear
Promotes more in-depth study because students must recall answers		May overestimate learning due to bluffing
Effective for assessing who, what, where, and when information		Generally limited to knowledge and comprehension questions
Relatively easy to construct		Not suitable for item analysis
Effective as either a written or oral assessment		Often criticized for encouraging rote memorization
Quicker for students to complete than multiple-choice questions		

Adapted from *Developing short answer items,* by B. J. Mandernach, 2003b. Retrieved, July 7, 2006, from www.park.edu/cetl/quicktips/shortanswer.html

Specificity. Another decision to make is the degree of specificity required in student responses. A potential problem with supply-type items is that a student may provide an answer that is technically correct but not the answer the teacher was looking for. If you want specific information to be provided by the student, the question can prompt for it. In the first example below, there is a range of possible responses that would work. In the second example below, it is clearer that the teacher is looking for a specific date (recall):

World War II started in _____.
World War II started in the year _____.

Hidden clues. Another problem with supply-type items is that the answers can sometimes be deduced from the way in which the question is written. For example, a definition may be included in the item, or the grammar structure provides the student with an unintended clue (e.g., plural version, gender, *a/an*). In the example below, the question contains an unintended clue to the answer because there simply aren't very many punctuation marks that start with a vowel:

The correct punctuation mark in sentence #4 is an _____.

Cloze procedure. In addition to using supply-type items on tests, educators can use them for reading assessments. The Cloze procedure is a technique in which words are deleted from a passage according to a word-count formula. The passage is presented to students, who insert words as they read to complete the text and construct meaning from it. This procedure can be used as a diagnostic reading assessment technique, to determine a student's independent reading level, and to check for understanding of content-area texts. It is especially helpful for content-area teachers who want to know if their reading assignments are too difficult for students or who want to check for understanding of a specific piece of text. The procedure for conducting a Cloze activity, included below, is fairly simple (McKenna & Robinson, 1980):

1. Select a piece of text and determine the grade level of the text (this can be done with the Fry Readability Formula or any number of published measures).
2. From this piece of text, select a representative 100-word passage.
3. Leave the first and last sentences and all of the punctuation intact.
4. Delete every fifth word of the remaining sentences. Replace these words with blank lines. Attempt to make all of the blank lines an equal length to avoid including visual clues about the lengths of omitted words.
5. Ask the student to read the entire passage and then reread the passage while writing in the missing words. No time limits are set.
6. Responses are correct even if misspelled, and each correct response is worth 2 points.
7. Score the assessment as follows: 57–100 points indicates an *independent* reading level for the student, 44–56 points indicates that this is the *instructional* level for the student, and less than 44 points indicates that the material is in the student's *frustrational* level (Shanker & Ekwall, 2003).

Once the results are tallied, you will have a general idea of where to begin instruction in this or a similar text. By examining the types of errors a student makes, you can determine the student's success in comprehending the passage as well as the instructional needs the specific student has.

Dichotomous Choices

Dichotomous-choice items, known commonly as true-or-false, can also be called alternative-response items or binary-choice items (Chatterji, 2003; Linn & Miller, 2005). Students are asked to identify if a declarative statement is true or false, if they agree or disagree, if it's right or wrong, if it's correct or incorrect, if it's a fact or opinion, or simply reply yes or no. The most common use of dichotomous choices is to determine if students understand the correctness of statements of fact, if they agree with opinions, if they can define terms, or if they can understand a principle. Advantages and disadvantages of dichotomous-choice items are listed in Figure 6.7.

Figure 6.7	Advantages and Disadvantages of Dichotomous-Choice Items	
Advantages		**Disadvantages**
Relatively easy to write and develop		May overestimate learning due to the influence of guessing
Quick to score		Difficult to differentiate between effective difficult items and trick items
Objective nature limits bias in scoring		Often leads to testing of trivial facts or bits of information
Easily administered to large numbers of students		Generally less discriminating than multiple-choice items
Effective as either a written or oral assessment		May not accurately reflect realistic circumstances in which issues are not absolutely true or false
Limits bias due to poor writing and/or reading skills		Often criticized for encouraging rote memorization
Highly efficient as large amount of knowledge can be sampled in a short amount of time		
Amenable to item analysis, which allows for improvement of the assessment device		

From *Quality true–false items,* by B. J. Mandernach, 2003d. Retrieved July 7, 2006, from www.park.edu/cetl/quicktips/truefalse.html

To be most effective in assessing specific learning objectives, dichotomous-choice tests should target only one fact per item. Doing so allows the teacher to determine whether or not the students understand the particular fact, idea, principle, or opinion.

In his U.S. history class, Robert Villarino uses weekly true/false tests to check for understanding. However, to increase the cognitive demand he places on his students, Mr. Villarino requires that students correct the false items. This requires students to move beyond the simple judgment of true or false and identify specific errors within the statement to demonstrate their understanding of the information. For example, on one of his weekly tests, Mr. Villarino wrote:

> Francis Scott Key, the writer of the "Star Spangled Banner," was a supporter of the War of 1812. TRUE / FALSE

Jessica got the question right by selecting false. However, that could have been a lucky guess. Her writing confirmed that she understood the information:

> Mr. Key said that this war (1812) was "a lump of wickedness" so, unless he is very sarcastic, he did not support the war.

Importantly, studies of dichotomous-choice items suggest that students tend to mark "true" when guessing; thus, false items tend to discriminate better between students who understand the information and those who do not. Having said that, we also know that students look for patterns in tests, consciously and subconsciously, so we caution you to balance the number of questions that are true with the number that are false.

Essays

Essay items, also known as extended-response items, are the most common type of performance assessment or task we ask students to complete (Johnson & Johnson, 2002; Linn & Miller, 2005). The essay requires that students consolidate their understanding of a topic, organize their thinking, and present it. While essays should not be overused, they do provide an opportunity for students to synthesize or evaluate information and are thus an excellent opportunity for teachers to check for understanding. A list of advantages and disadvantages of essay items can be found in Figure 6.8.

Figure 6.8	Advantages and Disadvantages of Essay Questions	
Advantages		**Disadvantages**
Encourage the organization of knowledge, integration of theories, and expression of opinions		Subjective scoring is less reliable, more time-consuming, and subject to bias
Promote original, novel thinking		Grading may be influenced by handwriting, length of response, and writing skills
Advantageous for assessing complex learning outcomes such as application, synthesis, and evaluation levels of understanding		Not effective in testing isolated facts or other lower-level cognitive objectives
Emphasize the ability to effectively communicate knowledge in a coherent fashion		More time-consuming to answer, so limited content can be assessed
Relatively easy to construct		May overestimate learning due to the influence of bluffing
Stimulate increased studying as students cannot answer via simple recognition		
Students are less likely to correctly guess answers without some prior knowledge		

Adapted from *Developing essay items,* by B. J. Mandernach, 2003a. Retrieved July 7, 2006, from www.park.edu/cetl/quicktips/essay.html

> As Criswell and Criswell (2004) note,
>
> Assessment reforms of the early '90s encouraged the development and use of "newer" forms of assessment including portfolios, performance tasks, and authentic assessments. As of late, however, there appears to be a regressive emphasis toward the use of objective item formats, especially in the area of state-mandated testing (Darling-Hammond, 2003). Despite shifts in assessment theory, the essay item format remained a credible and fundamental tool for assessing student achievement. (p. 510)

The essay endures because it is helpful in checking for understanding and allowing students to consolidate their thinking.

In terms of general guidelines for the development of essay items, teachers are cautioned to note the amount of time required to grade and carefully evaluate student work. While there are a number of computerized programs being developed to help teachers score essays, some of which are getting fairly reliable (Koul, Clariana, & Salehi, 2005), checking for understanding and linking assessment findings with instruction require that teachers understand the thinking of students.

In addition, there is evidence that essay grading is somewhat subjective (Blok, 1985; Wang, 2000). Sometimes subjectivity is introduced because the item is ambiguous or open to significant personal interpretation. To address this area of bias, teachers must construct items carefully and ensure that there is sufficient focus to the question.

Another way subjectivity is introduced involves the administration of the item. Students need to understand the time limits for the item, the weighting of each item (how much of the grade it is worth), and the scoring criteria that will be used. As with all types of rubrics, developing the scoring criteria with students and ensuring that students understand the criteria before participating in the assessment will result in a more accurate picture of their knowledge and allow the teacher to use this information to check for understanding (Mertler, 2001; Skillings & Ferrell, 2000).

A final concern in terms of the subjectivity and bias in essay tests involves the prior knowledge the teacher has about the student and whether or not the teacher can hold that information in check while reading and scoring a specific piece of writing. Teachers can reduce this "halo effect" by grading essays without knowing the identity of the student. Some teachers fold over the corner of the front page and then mix up the papers; others implement a coding system to ensure that they are not biased in their review.

Ninth grade English teacher Chip Stroehlein's students study big ideas and essential questions. The books they read are connected to these bigger ideas. Mr. Stroehlein reads one book aloud to the class that he selects based on the theme or big idea. Students in his classes choose books connected with the theme and then read and discuss these books in literature circles. This allows Mr. Stroehlein to differentiate reading materials and meet student needs while also ensuring that the entire class is able to have a conversation on a bigger idea that matters.

During a unit titled "What's Love Got to Do with It?" Mr. Stroehlein read *Romeo and Juliet* aloud to his students. Upon finishing Act III, he asked his students to respond to the following essay question:

When she finds Juliet weeping, Lady Capulet assumes that Juliet is still mourning over Tybalt's death. Explain why Shakespeare gives Juliet lines filled with double meanings. Support your ideas with at least two details from the text.

Mr. Stroehlein uses his students' responses to check their understanding of the book they are engaged with as a whole class. He asks other questions of his students to check their understanding of the books they are reading in their literature circles and still other questions to ensure that his students are engaged with the essential question.

Similarly, fourth grade teacher Shayne Peterson uses an essay to check his students' understanding of *Tales of a Fourth Grade Nothing* (Blume, 1972). At one point, Mr. Peterson provided students with the prompt found in Figure 6.9. A sample of Armando's margin notes is shown in Figure 6.10; Figure 6.11 shows his response to the essay item. When Mr. Peterson read Armando's paper, he knew that Armando was making connections with the text. He could tell from the student's response to the essay question that he understood the idea of the unit on personal connections. He also noted that Armando's English proficiency continued to increase. Because Armando had only been in U.S. schools for 17 months, Mr. Peterson expected a number of interlinguistic errors in Armando's writing. However, he noted that Armando seemed to understand the generally accepted format for essay writing and had made significant improvement in his spelling; the teacher also identified the grammar rules that still seemed to confuse Armando.

Figure 6.9	Fourth-Grade Writing Prompt

Writing Situation
When we read, our thoughts, ideas, and feelings interact with the author's. We may wonder why a character acts a certain way or what will happen next. The piece may relate to our own lives in some way, so it might cause us to remember the past or to think about the future. This is called responding to literature.

Directions for Writing
Read the passage from *Tales of a Fourth Grade Nothing* by Judy Blume. In the margins, make notes of your responses as you read. Use these notes to help you with your writing.

Write a piece that describes your response to the passage and what parts of it produced that response. Relate any ideas or events from the story to your own life. Be sure to finish up with a summary paragraph that contains the main ideas of your response.

Figure 6.10	Armando's Margin Notes

don't lick you or anything. Still, I had my very own pet at last.

Later, when I sat down at the dinner table, my mother said, "I smell turtle. Peter, go and *scrub* your hands!"

Some people might think that my mother is my biggest problem. She doesn't like turtles and she's always telling me to scrub my hands. That doesn't mean just run them under the water. *Scrub* means I'm supposed to use soap and rub my hands together. Then I've got to rinse and dry them. I ought to know by now, I've heard it enough!

But my mother isn't my biggest problem. Neither is my father. He spends a lot of time watching commercials on TV. That's because he's in the advertising business. These days his favorite commercial is the one about Juicy-O. He wrote it himself. And the president of the Juicy-O company liked it so much he sent my father a whole crate of Juicy-O for our family to drink. It tastes like a combination of oranges, pineapples, grapefruits, pears, and bananas. (And if you want to know the truth, I'm getting pretty sick of drinking it.) But Juicy-O isn't my biggest problem either.

My biggest problem is my brother, Farley Drexel Hatcher. He's two-and-a-half years old. Everybody calls him Fudge. I feel sorry for him if he's going to grow up with a name like Fudge, but I don't say a word. It's none of my business.

Fudge is always in my way. He messes up everything he sees. And when he gets mad he throws himself flat on the floor and he screams. And he kicks. And he bangs his fist. The only time I really like him is when he's sleeping. He sucks four fingers on his left hand and makes a slurping noise.

When Fudge saw Dribble he said, "Ohhhh...see!"

And I said, "That's my turtle, get it? Mine! You don't touch him."

Fudge said, "No touch." Then he laughed like crazy.

The Important Details are:

Sometimes I do like to my mom always tells me "go wash your hands because you were touching that lizzard."

That's what my dad always do he spends his time watching commercial on the couch.

my sister is my problem because she always bother me. She even's break all my stuff in my room. That's what she did when she saw the lizzard.

Figure 6.11	Armando's Summary

Test #23
6/29/04
12 7 3

①

<u>Summary</u>

In the beggining of the story I felt Suprised because he was almost related to me. One time I won a lizzard and my mom reacted the same way when you said "my mother made a face." So she was not Suprised.

next I brought the lizzard Inside. I even have Some one who takes me to places and knows my name and that know what grade I am In. So I said the same thing when she asked me who Is going to take care of It.

Finally I said "I am the one who is going to take care of It so she let my keep the lizzard. But She Said "It will be yours responsibility taking care of that turtle. She even said I Haded to clean his cage feed him and be a good owner to that pet. So I went to my room and put him on my top shelf.

Conclusion

As Tomlinson (1999) so aptly states, "Assessment always has more to do with helping students grow than with cataloging their mistakes" (p. 11). We couldn't agree more. Tests and assessments can and should be used to check for understanding with the goal of increasingly precise instruction for individual students. Although we acknowledge that tests and assessments will be used for other purposes—report cards, grading, and public accountability, to name a few—it is critical that we also use the information we gather through testing to plan our instruction.

7

Using Common Assessments and Consensus Scoring to Check for Understanding

When teachers in course-alike groups or grade-level teams meet on a regular basis to look at student work, checking for understanding becomes a systemwide process. Like the authors of *Collaborative Analysis of Student Work* (Langer, Colton, & Goff, 2003) and *Common Formative Assessments* (Ainsworth & Viegut, 2006), in this chapter we explore the ways that teacher teams can use assessment information to guide their instructional interventions. We expand on this work by providing evidence of how important it is for teachers to use common assessments as part of the school's professional learning community. We also describe ways in which teachers can use consensus scoring to increase their expectations, tune the curriculum, and inform instruction.

Using Data to Improve Student Achievement[1]

There are a number of strategies that can be used to improve student achievement and close the achievement gap, including hiring veteran teachers, purchasing new curricula, providing after-school tutoring, and so on. These are all likely to have positive effects on the achievement of students who are performing at less than

[1] Portions of this chapter appeared previously in "Using data to improve student achievement," by D. Fisher and C. Johnson, 2006, *Principal Leadership*, 7(2), 27–31. Used with permission from the National Association of Secondary School Principals. For more information, see www.nassp.org.

acceptable levels. Our experience, however, suggests that it is the teacher and what the teacher does that makes the difference for students (Frey & Fisher, 2006). We know that access to professional development differentiates teachers who have the knowledge and skills to meet the increasing demands of our diverse student population and those who do not (Joyce & Showers, 2002). We also know that not all professional development is created equally (National Staff Development Council, 2001). Teachers deserve professional development that is engaging, based on current research evidence, aligned with standards, and provides them opportunities for peer engagement.

Understanding this, we have developed and implemented a protocol for examining and aligning content standards, creating common assessments, scoring student work by consensus, and planning changes based on the information gathered in this process. Let's explore the protocol first and then look at the results of the protocol in checking for understanding and in closing the achievement gap.

A Protocol for Using Common Assessments

There are a number of recursive steps that can be used to align curriculum, instruction, and assessment such that student learning becomes the focus of professional development and teachers can check for understanding at the grade or department level.

Step 1: Pacing Guides

The first step in the process involves gathering teachers with common courses (e.g., 3rd grade, 7th grade English, U.S. history, algebra) to meet and decide on a timeline for the sequence of content instruction. The group of teachers will need access to their content standards to ensure that each standard is addressed in a meaningful way. While this sounds easy, it can be the most difficult part of the protocol. Some teachers may resist standards-aligned instruction; others may have their favorite units or teaching order. Still others may be unfamiliar with their content standards and the expectations of their specific grade level. It is hard to imagine a way to close the achievement gap if students do not have access to instruction that is aligned with the grade-level standards.

Step 2: Instructional Materials and Arrangements

Once pacing guides have been agreed upon, teachers must select instructional materials, strategies, approaches, and arrangements. While the materials may be selected for teachers in many states, they know that they can use the materials in a variety of ways. In discussions during this step in the protocol, teachers share their evidence-based and effective instructional approaches with one another. In addition, the team may request assistance from a consultant who has more information about instructional strategies and approaches. In this way, the work of the consultant is contextualized in the work of the teacher teams.

Step 3: Common Assessments

At predetermined points in the school year, but no less than every six weeks, students should participate in a common assessment of their learning. While there are a number of commercially available tests and assessments, our experience suggests that when groups of teachers create their own common assessments, scores rise faster. Creating an assessment, even an imperfect one, allows groups of teachers to talk about the standards, how the standards might be assessed, where students are performing currently, and what learning needs to take place for students to demonstrate proficiency. In other words, creating common assessments provides teachers with an opportunity to "begin with the end in mind" (Covey, 2004). In addition, common assessments provide students with test format practice, which has been documented to increase performance (Langer, 2001). When students understand the genre of the test, they are likely to do better.

Step 4: Consensus Scoring and Item Analysis

Once all of the students have participated in the common assessment and the results have been tabulated, teachers should meet to discuss the results. The results are presented for the grade or course, not for individual teachers. The results are also disaggregated by significant subpopulations, such as students with disabilities, students who are English language learners, or specific ethnic/racial groups. This allows teachers to identify and discuss achievement gaps and plan interventions.

When considering a specific item, teachers note the number or percentage of students who answered correctly and hypothesize why the students who answered incorrectly did so. They question one another about students' understandings and misunderstandings and theorize about future instruction, pacing, instructional materials, assessments, and planning.

Step 5: Revising Pacing Guides, Reviewing Assessments, Reteaching, and Forming Intervention Groups

As noted in Step 4, as teachers review student work they note changes that need to be made in the pacing guides, review standards for clarification of the content, and plan for reteaching opportunities. Teachers also discuss the implications that specific instructional materials have for students' learning and make recommendations about changes in this aspect. In some schools, teachers request the assessment data for their own students so that they can compare with the school, department, or grade average. This final step provides an opportunity for the protocol to cycle again; the assessment data inform instruction, curriculum, and future assessments. Along the way, gaps in student performance are identified and plans are developed to address these gaps, whether they be between ethnic/racial groups or between the students and the state content standards. The teacher may choose to meet with certain groups of students on a temporary basis, providing instruction on the missing subject knowledge or skills. In high-performing schools, gaps in student knowledge are often addressed in after-school programs such as the federally funded 21st Century Community Learning Centers. Thus, common assessments become the link between the school day and the after-school interventions.

The Protocol in Action

We have begun using this protocol in the City Heights Educational Collaborative, a partnership between San Diego State University and three public schools: Rosa Parks Elementary, Monroe Clark Middle School, and Hoover High School. These three schools serve more than 5,300 students collectively. Of these 5,300 students, 99.5 percent qualify for free or reduced-priced lunch and 76 percent are English language learners who are native speakers of one of 39 different languages. Rita Elwardi and Lee Mongrue, teachers at Hoover High School, developed the tools in Figure 7.1 to track the progress teacher teams made as they implemented this protocol. The following three examples of checking for understanding using common assessments and consensus scoring represent the outcomes of this protocol. We selected these examples from the many we have to highlight the use of checking for understanding in a systemwide manner. We selected these examples from different content areas and grade levels—middle school English language arts, high school history, and elementary school math—to show the versatility of the protocol.

Improving Middle School Writing

The protocol was used at Monroe Clark Middle School to improve writing scores (Fisher, Lapp, & Flood, 2005). Teachers in grades 6, 7, and 8 met to discuss their writing curriculum. They noted several deficiencies: they did not have a common language for writing genres; they did not teach the genres that were specifically addressed in the California middle school standards; and they did not have all of the instructional tools they needed to ensure that their students would become stronger communicators. Once they agreed on a pacing guide for their writing instruction, they created writing prompts based on the types of writing described in the state standards. These writing prompts, given every seven weeks to all students, were scored by consensus and discussed to understand any instructional implications of the scores. In California, 7th graders take a state writing assessment that is scored by two readers on a scale of 1 to 4. The lowest score an individual student can receive is 2, and the highest score is 8. After using the protocol for just a few years, students clearly showed marked improvement in writing achievement, as shown in Figure 7.2.

Improving High School History Knowledge

At the high school level, the protocol was used by a group of five teachers who all teach the same course. The teachers met regularly to discuss their content standards and the ways in which those content standards can be assessed. They regularly administer a common assessment that includes 10 to 12 questions. They also use writing prompts and interviews to explore students' thinking about the content. On a recent common assessment, the following question was used:

For what purpose did Parliament vote during the Restoration?
A. To restore Puritan religion in England
B. To restore the monarchy in England

Figure 7.1	Tools for Implementing the Common Assessment Protocol

Weekly Course-Alike Meeting	
Course:	**Date:**
Lead teacher or facilitator:	
Teachers in attendance:	

Focus: (indicate one)
☐ Curriculum pacing guide
☐ Strategy implementation
☐ Coaching practice
☐ Consensus scoring cycle
    ○ Common assessment development
    ○ Item analysis (See reverse side. Do not complete remainder of this page.)

Discussion points:	**Questions raised:**
Objective for the coming week:	**Resources needed:**

Implementation steps:

Figure 7.1	Tools for Implementing the Common Assessment Protocol (*continued*)
Item Analysis Summary	
Assessment tool:	
Student work: Areas of strength	
Student work: Areas of weakness	
Teacher practice: What should be preserved?	
Teacher practice: Identify gaps between existing and desired practice.	
Teacher practice: What aspects of existing practice pose a barrier to implementing desired practice?	
Teacher practice: Suggested interventions or unit modifications	
Unanswered questions:	

Adapted by R. Elwardi and L. Mongrue from *Smaller learning communities: Implementing and deepening practice,* by D. Oxley, 2005, Portland, OR: Northwest Regional Educational Laboratory.

Figure 7.2	Improved Writing Achievement Scores		
Score	In 2001	In 2004	Difference
8	0%	1%	+1%
6–7	5%	19%	+14%
4–5	18%	58%	+40%
2–3	78%	22%	−56%

C. To restore Charles I to power

D. To restore the idea of the divine right of kings

In terms of responses, 37.5 percent of the students chose A, 7.5 percent chose B (the correct answer), 17.5 percent chose C, and 37.5 percent chose D. While we might debate the relative merit of the question or the importance of this point in the overall understanding of history, the teachers noted that this is the type of question that confuses students on the state assessment and that this type of question is commonly asked of students on these assessments.

Having acknowledged this result, the conversation that the teachers had about this one question illustrates the power of this process. One of the teachers explained, "Restoration is when they brought the king back. I never really discussed the fact that Parliament voted on this. I really focus on the timeline, not so much why. Using the timeline, my students know that Oliver Cromwell ruined arts and literature and that Charles II restored them. I think that I missed one of the keys here, that Parliament restored the monarchy and ended the military dictatorship."

Another teacher focused on students' seeming lack of test-taking skills. He said, "Our students should have been able to delete several items right away. Charles I was beheaded, so C can't be right. Also, the divine right of kings is a belief system, not something that Parliament could or could not restore. They should have crossed those two choices off right away. We have to go back and review some common test-taking skills."

In terms of evidence that this systems works at the high school, the number of students receiving *F* grades in their history course dropped by 20 percent, and the number of students receiving an *A* or a *B* increased by 25 percent. Additionally, student performance on the state content standards assessment improved, as shown in Figure 7.3.

Figure 7.3	Improvement in Performance on State Standard in World History		
Performance Level	In 2002	In 2005	Difference
Advanced	0%	2%	+2%
Proficient	3%	9%	+6%
Basic	27%	31%	+4%
Below Basic	24%	22%	−2%
Far Below Basic	46%	36%	−10%

Improving Mathematics Achievement at the Elementary School

Math achievement at Rosa Parks Elementary School in 1999 was not impressive, to say the least. Students did not perform well and teachers were frustrated. The school educates over 1,560 students, 100 percent of whom qualified for free and reduced-price lunch, and 76 percent of whom were English language learners. Figures 7.4, 7.5, and 7.6 show the lack of mathematical understanding students had and how much has changed over the years. Dr. Donna Kopenski, math resource teacher at Rosa Parks, has led the curriculum development and common assessment process at the school for several years. She describes the process and conversations teachers have as they check for understanding as grade-level teams. Also note that teachers plan instructional interventions and curriculum revisions as a result of their discussions and review of student work.

Figure 7.4	Changes in Math Achievement by Grade		
Grade	Proficient/Advanced in 1999	Proficient/Advanced in 2005	Difference
2	21%	64%	+43%
3	12%	58%	+46%
4	15%	55%	+40%
5	19%	47%	+28%

Figure 7.5	Math Achievement in All Grades 2–5	
School Year		**Proficient/Advanced**
2001–02		25.8%
2002–03		31.8%
2003–04		43.1%
2004–05		56.3%

Figure 7.6	Percent of Proficient/Advanced Students in 2005 As Compared with District and State Scores			
Grade	**Rosa Parks**	**District**	**State**
2	64%	61%	56%
3	58%	57%	54%
4	55%	52%	50%
5	48%	44%	44%

To check for their students' understanding using a common assessment, the 3rd grade teachers analyzed individual items on the test. First, they correlated the items with content standards and identified items aligned with key standards that fewer than 60 percent of students answered correctly. Next, they identified items aligned with non-key standards that had fewer than 60 percent correct responses. There were four key standards and seven non-key standards associated with items that fewer than 60 percent of students got correct. The teachers then checked to see how many questions were asked for each standard and considered each question on the test for discussion.

Using the standards analysis, the teachers discovered that the key standard with the lowest percent correct was in the area of measurement and geometry. Standard MG 1.3 reads: "Find the perimeter of a polygon with integer sides." There were two items on the assessment that addressed this standard: one item showed a rectangle with the length and width labeled, and the second item showed a rectangle with squares filled in and no measurements given. Although 76.6 percent of the students selected the correct answer for the first item, only 28.9 percent answered the second item correctly. Even more puzzling was the fact that 48.1 percent of the students chose the same incorrect response to the second item. Figure 7.7 shows this second item.

Figure 7.7	Common Assessment Item of Concern, 3rd Grade

47. Each floor tile is 1 foot square. What is the perimeter of the floor?

A. 11 ft
B. 22 ft
C. 29 ft
D. 26 ft

The teachers determined that the question was valid and simply stated. The next step was to look at the distractors. It soon became apparent to the teachers that the students who chose C (48.1 percent) were most likely trying to find the *area* by counting the squares or multiplying 5 × 6 and chose the answer 29 because it was closest to the area (30 sq ft). Another suggestion was that when the students saw the grid with all the little squares they immediately thought of area since that is how they usually see the area questions presented in the text. The teachers were still confused as to why the students had a difficult time finding the perimeter. After much discussion, the group came to the consensus that they really needed to work on teaching perimeter in various ways, especially when a grid is given with no values.

In a similar fashion, Rosa Parks's 5th grade teachers analyzed common math assessment items and also spent a great deal of time unpacking the curriculum and revising the pacing guide. Fifth grade has a larger number of mathematics standards, and the growth has not been as great as it has been in 3rd grade. The 5th grade teachers found that there were five key standards in which fewer than 60 percent of students selected the correct choice; of those five, four were in the area of measurement and geometry. This was of great concern to the teachers because it was apparent that it was a weak area. Let's consider an item representing key standard MG 1.2: "Construct a cube and rectangular box from two-dimensional patterns and use these patterns to compute the surface area for these objects." See Figure 7.8.

Figure 7.8	Common Assessment Item, 5th Grade

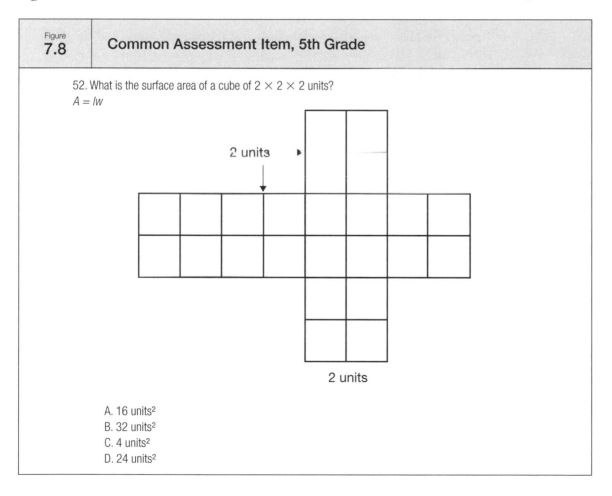

52. What is the surface area of a cube of $2 \times 2 \times 2$ units?
$A = lw$

2 units

2 units

A. 16 units²
B. 32 units²
C. 4 units²
D. 24 units²

The interesting thing about this problem is that 22.7 percent of the students chose answer A, 23.8 percent chose C, and 42.7 percent chose D (the correct response). The teachers were at a loss to explain how the students came up with a response of 16 units, but they guessed that some students chose 4 units because they added (or multiplied) the 2 units and 2 units that were on the illustration. The group felt that the question was valid but wondered if there was too much information given, confusing the students. Determining what information is needed to solve a problem was definitely a strategy that needed emphasis. The 5th grade teachers also agreed that they needed to do more work with surface area in general.

In the fall of each school year, an all-day meeting is held for each grade level to discuss only mathematics. At that meeting, data regarding common assessments are distributed to the teachers and time is taken to evaluate test items and to work on strategies for teaching difficult concepts. If teachers did not have all the data on each item and were not given the time to compare the data and examine the items in question, they would never really know what their students understood or how they could better instruct their students. The teachers at all grade levels have expressed how much they value the time to meet and discuss their grade-level content.

Conclusion

Our short glimpses into the regular discussions these teachers have highlight a number of important issues related to improving student achievement through checking for understanding. First, teachers must understand their content standards. Some of the best professional development related to content standards happens when groups of teachers attempt to create common assessment items from the standards. Second, when teachers analyze students' responses to test items, they gain a greater understanding of students' thinking and can use that information in their instruction. Third, when groups of students clearly do not understand content information, teachers can intervene. Using this protocol, teachers have the information they need to form intervention groups and do not have to wait until the school year is over to find out who needed additional help on which standards.

Creating systems for teachers to engage with their peers and administrators in systematically looking at student work, supported with collaboratively developed pacing guides and common assessments, can help close the achievement gap that has persisted for decades. We do not need to change teachers to get the results our students deserve. Instead, we need to focus our professional development on ensuring that teachers understand their grade-level and content-specific standards, how those standards are assessed, and what to do when students do not perform well. This will create the breakthrough that Fullan, Hill, and Crévola (2006) talk about. Through peer support and collegial conversations, we can fulfill the promise of public education—access to a quality adult life in a democratic society.

Afterword

Checking Your Own Understanding

This book has been about checking students' understanding as they learn content and performance objectives. But it is also about the implications of checking for understanding on our own classroom and schoolwide practices, especially with regard to reflective teaching and collaboration with our colleagues. To borrow a term from Wiggins and McTighe, we offer a few of our own "enduring understandings" about the process as it relates to teaching, learning, and school reform efforts.

Checking for Understanding Fosters Good Teaching

The most immediate benefit of checking for understanding in the classroom is that it results in improved teaching. Old (and ineffective) habits associated with relying on an Initiate-Respond-Evaluate cycle of questioning are supplanted when teachers use questioning to determine what is known and unknown. Students' verbal and written responses are valued because they provide a window into the minds of learners by answering the teacher's perpetual question: What is the next instructional move?

Teachers who regularly check for understanding appreciate the need to get responses from all students, not just the ones who know the answer. After all, this process makes it clear that understanding can't be adequately checked when only a few responses are considered. In too many classrooms, a tacit agreement between teacher and students is maintained: I'll ask the questions, a few of you will answer for the entire class, and we'll all pretend this is the same as learning. A teacher who checks for understanding seeks responses from students who do not commonly raise their hands. Checking for understanding means viewing work samples, providing opportunities for performance, and broadening the definition of testing and assessment beyond a grade-giving function.

Checking for Understanding Fosters Metacognition

When teachers become more deliberate in the ways they check for understanding, they model the metacognitive awareness learners need to develop. Metacognition is the ability of learners to "predict their performances on various tasks . . . and to monitor their current levels of mastery and understanding" (National Research Council, 2000, p. 12). While it may appear that checking for understanding is a teacher-centered strategy, in truth, it empowers students to take responsibility for their own learning through monitoring and goal setting. When teachers make checking for understanding a routine part of the learning environment, they demonstrate the many ways in which to recognize that learning has occurred. Importantly, the teacher who checks for understanding transmits the message that the goal of the classroom is not just to get a good grade but also to learn (National Research Council, 2000).

Checking for Understanding Encourages Looking for Multiple Representations of Knowledge

The process of checking for understanding requires that teachers move beyond asking questions and giving tests to determine whether learning has occurred. Many of the routine practices of schooling take on new possibilities in the hands of a skilled educator. Written work and projects offer evidence of the ways in which a student is learning, not just a simple measure of the volume of learning. A teacher who seeks to check for understanding creates new opportunities for students to demonstrate their learning. When the teacher knows that he or she cannot just pause occasionally during a lecture to ask, "Any questions?" the teacher must ensure that students are given ways to reply in writing, such as summary writing of a key concept or developing a graphic organizer of the relationships between concepts. The teacher incorporates projects, portfolios, and performances into the routine of the classroom. Over time, students learn that there is more than one way to demonstrate their learning and more than one way to monitor their own understanding.

Checking for Understanding Deepens Assessment

In traditional classrooms, assessment is narrowly defined as a testing function. Student learning is routinely measured as a summative measure, with relatively little attention afforded to incremental appraisals of progress toward learning goals. Students view these events with anxiety, knowing that they need to perform well in order to earn a good grade. The world is thus divided into right and wrong answers, and learning is equated with the ability to memorize, recall, and regurgitate information on demand.

In classrooms where assessment and testing are used to check for understanding, teachers are clear about the purposes for these events. Students come to expect that their teachers will regularly ask them about what they know so far in order to make instructional decisions. In departments and grade levels where common assessments are given, learners hear the language of reflective teaching. They know their teachers will meet to discuss the results of the assessments and talk about instruction. It is possible that in such classrooms, students will hear their teachers explain why they are teaching the lesson and what they hope to accomplish. Because teachers who use common assessments collaborate to create these measures, they develop greater clarity about their purposes for teaching and how understanding can be assessed.

Checking for Understanding Is Aligned with Best Practices

A final advantage in checking for understanding is that it is aligned with many of the best practices associated with planning, instruction, and school reform.

First, checking for understanding demands that one knows what is worth checking. As Wiggins and McTighe (2005) note, understanding is more than just "knowing" something; it is the ability to apply what is known to a new situation or task. Checking for understanding ultimately involves knowing what the enduring understandings of a lesson should be and what knowledge, skills, and strategies are needed to progress to that level. Planning then necessarily includes the learning that will be assessed and the methods that best accomplish that learning.

Checking for understanding is critical to differentiating instruction (Tomlinson, 1999). In a differentiated classroom, content, process, and product are aligned to student strengths and needs, allowing each learner to operate in an optimal learning environment. Therefore, the teacher must have a clear understanding of the ways in which each student will demonstrate his or her progress toward mastery. Tomlinson compares this to conducting an orchestra, with players working on different sections of the score. The role of the teacher is to achieve a balance and harmony across the players so that those enduring understandings are achieved by all, resulting in a successful performance.

Finally, checking for understanding is consistent with school reform efforts that seek to link instruction and assessment in meaningful ways. Fullan, Hill, and Crévola's (2006) call for "expert systems" in schools offers clear connections to the classroom. They define expert systems as "two key subsystems. One is the knowledge base about what experts do in particular situations; the other is the case-specific data that relates to the situation at hand. Experts are nothing without data on current status" (p. 47). This perspective has two implications for school reform: first, with regard to what will serve as the knowledge base and the data to be examined; and second, with respect to what ways teachers and administrators will have opportunities to analyze, synthesize, and evaluate that information. Therefore, checking for understanding is useful at the school level as well as in classroom instruction. As a practice, checking for understanding should be a model for the ways in which we collaborate with our colleagues.

Checking Your Own Understanding

Tomlinson's comparison of teaching and learning to the tasks of an orchestra leader is useful when thinking about our own professional learning. Ultimately, checking for understanding is not a hierarchical or linear set of strategies and procedures. While we have arranged this book according to the constructs associated with classroom teaching, the strategies for checking for understanding become richer when considered across domains. Oral language, for instance, has everything to do with questioning, writing, performance, and so on. Wiggins and McTighe (2005) explain that enduring understandings are those that can be transferred to new situations and tasks. Tomlinson (1999) writes that effective teachers "seek varied means of assessment so that all students can fully display their skills and understandings" (p. 11). And Fullan and colleagues (2006) note that expert systems require both a knowledge base and data with which to apply that knowledge base to a new situation. In order to advance your own comprehension of checking for understanding, it is necessary to monitor your learning, reflect on its implications, and engage with colleagues in analyzing both instructional practice and the data that are yielded from such efforts. To this end, we have included a note-taking guide (see Figure A.1) for you to record your knowledge about strategies used to check for understanding. In addition, we have created an online study guide (visit www.ascd.org/studyguides) for you and your department, grade level, or school to use as you expand your efforts to check for understanding.

Figure A.1	Checking for Understanding Strategy Grid

1. Oral Language

Strategy	Description	How I Can Use It
Accountable talk		
Noticing nonverbal cues		
Value lineups		
Retellings		
Think-Pair-Share		
Misconception analysis		
Whip around		

2. Questioning

Strategy	Description	How I Can Use It
Constructing effective questions		
Providing nonverbal support		
Developing authentic questions		
Response cards		
Hand signals		
Audience response systems		
ReQuest		
Socratic seminar		

3. Writing

Strategy	Description	How I Can Use It
Interactive writing		
Read-Write-Pair-Share		
Summary writing		
RAFT		

Figure A.1	Checking for Understanding Strategy Grid (continued)

4. Projects and Performances

Strategy	Description	How I Can Use It
Readers' Theatre		
Multimedia presentations		
Electronic and paper portfolios		
Graphic organizers		
Inspiration		
Foldables		
Dioramas		
Public performances		

5. Tests

Strategy	Description	How I Can Use It
Multiple-choice items		
Short-answer items		
Dichotomous choices		
Essays		

6. Common Assessments

Strategy	Description	How I Can Use It
Pacing guides		
Instructional materials and arrangements		
Common assessments		
Consensus scoring and item analysis		
Revising pacing guides, reviewing assessments, reteaching, and forming intervention groups		

References

Adams, C. (2004). *Guidelines for participants in a Socratic seminar.* Vestivia Hills High School, Birmingham, AL.

Adler, D. A. (1992). *A picture book of Harriet Tubman.* New York: Holiday House.

Ainsworth, L., & Viegut, D. (2006). *Common formative assessments: How to connect standards-based instruction and assessment.* Thousand Oaks, CA: Corwin

Armstrong, S., & Warlick, D. (2004). The new literacy: The 3 Rs evolve into the 4 Es. *Technology and Learning, 25*(2), 20–24.

Bainton, G. (1890). *The art of authorship: Literary reminiscences, methods of work, and advice to young beginners, personally contributed by leading authors of the day.* London: J. Clark and Co.

Barrett, H. C. (2006). *Required high school portfolios.* Retrieved July 8, 2006, from http://electronicportfolios.org/blog/2006_06_14detail.html

Barron, B. J. S., Schwartz, D. L., Vye, N. J., Moore, A., Petrosino, A., Zech, L., et al. (1998). Doing with understanding: Lessons from research on problem and project-based learning. *The Journal of the Learning Sciences, 7*(3/4), 271–311.

Beck, I., McKeown, M., Hamilton, R., & Kucan, L. (1997). *Questioning the author: An approach for enhancing student engagement with text.* Newark, DE: International Reading Association.

Bennett, A., Bridgall, B. L., Cauce, A. M., Everson, H. T., Gordon, E. W., Lee, C. D., et al. (2004). *All students reaching the top: Strategies for closing academic achievement gaps.* Naperville, IL: Learning Point Associates, North Central Regional Educational Laboratory.

Biemiller, A. (1999). *Language and reading success.* Brookline, MA: Brookline Books.

Blok, H. (1985). Estimating the reliability, validity, and invalidity of essay ratings. *Journal of Educational Measurement, 22*(1), 41–52.

Bloom, B. S. (1956). *Taxonomy of educational objectives: The classification of educational goals: Handbook I, Cognitive domain.* New York: Longman.

Bloom, B. S., & Broder, L. J. (1950). *Problem-solving processes of college students: An exploratory investigation.* Chicago: University of Chicago Press.

Blume, J. (1972). *Tales of a fourth grade nothing.* New York: Dutton.

Bremer, J., & Bodley, B. (2004). Multimedia madness: Creating with a purpose. *Library Media Connection, 23*(2), 31–33.

Brophy, J. (1990). Teaching social studies for understanding and higher-order application. *The Elementary School Journal, 90,* 351–417.

Brophy, J., & Alleman, J. (2002). Learning and teaching about cultural universals in primary-grade social studies. *The Elementary School Journal, 103*(2), 99–114.

Brophy, J. E., & Evertson, C. M. (1974). *Texas teacher effectiveness project: Final report.* (Research Rep. No. 74-4). Austin, TX: University of Texas.

Bye, E., & Johnson, K. K. P. (2004). Writing-to-learn in the apparel curriculum. *Journal of Family and Consumer Sciences, 96,* 43–47.

Calero, H. H. (2005). *The power of non-verbal communication: What you do is more important than what you say.* Lansdowne, PA: Silver Lake Publishing.

Callella, T., & Jordano, K. (2002). *Interactive writing: Students and teachers "sharing the pen" to create meaningful text.* Huntington Beach, CA: Creative Teaching Press.

Cambourne, B. (1998). *Read and retell.* Melbourne, Australia: Nelson.

Carlson, C. (2000). Scientific literacy for all. *The Science Teacher, 67*(3), 48–52.

Cassidy, J. (1989). Using graphic organizers to develop critical thinking. *Gifted Child Today, 12*(6), 34–36.

Cazden, C. B. (1988). *Classroom discourse: The language of teaching and learning.* Portsmouth, NH: Heinemann.

CCCC Committee on Assessment. (1995). Writing assessment: A position statement. *College Composition and Communication, 46,* 430–437.

Chatterji, M. (2003). *Designing and using tools for educational assessment.* Boston: Allyn and Bacon.

Christenbury, L. (2006). *Making the journey: Being and becoming a teacher of English language arts.* Portsmouth, NH: Heinemann.

Cisneros, S. (1991). *Woman hollering creek, and other stories.* New York: Random House.

Clay, M. M. (2001). *Change over time in children's literacy development.* Portsmouth, NH: Heinemann.

Cohen, E. (1994). Restructuring the classroom: Conditions for productive small groups. *Review of Educational Research, 64*(1), 1–35.

Cooper, P., & Morreale, S. (Eds.). (2003). *Creating competent communicators: Activities for teaching speaking, listening, and media literacy in K–6 classrooms.* Scottsdale, AZ: Holcomb Hathaway.

Costa, A. L., & Kallick, B. (Eds.). (2000). *Discovering and exploring habits of mind.* Alexandria, VA: Association for Supervision and Curriculum Development.

Cotton, K. (1989). Expectations and student outcomes. Portland, OR: Northwest Regional Educational Laboratory. Available: www.nwrel.org/scpd/sirs/4/cu7.html

Covey, S. R. (2004). *The 7 habits of highly effective people: Powerful lessons in personal change* (Rev. ed.). New York: Free Press.

Criswell, J. R., & Criswell, S. J. (2004). Asking essay questions: Answering contemporary needs. *Education, 124,* 510–516.

Curtis, C. P. (1995). *The Watsons go to Birmingham—1963.* New York: Delacorte Press.

Darling-Hammond, L. (2003). Standards and assessments: Where we are and what we need. *Teacher's College Record.* Available: http://www.tcrecord.org/content.asp?ContentID=11109

dePaola, T. (1973). *Nana upstairs and Nana downstairs.* New York: Putnam.

Dodge, B. (1998). *Schools, skills and scaffolding on the Web.* Retrieved July 6, 2006, from http://edweb.sdsu.edu/people/bdodge/scaffolding.html

Doherty, J., & Coggeshall, K. (2005). Reader's theater and storyboarding: Strategies that include and improve. *Voices from the Middle, 12*(4), 37–43.

Durkin, D. (1978). What classroom observation reveals about reading comprehension instruction. *Reading Research Quarterly, 14*(4), 481–533.

Dye, G. A. (2000). Graphic organizers to the rescue! Helping students link—and remember—information. *TEACHING Exceptional Children, 32*(3), 72–76.

Edens, K. M., & Potter, E. (2003). Using descriptive drawings as a conceptual change strategy in elementary science. *School Science and Mathematics, 103*(3), 135–144.

Egan, M. (1999). Reflections on effective use of graphic organizers. *Journal of Adolescent and Adult Literacy, 42,* 641–645.

Elbow, P. (1994). *Writing for learning—not just for demonstrating learning.* Retrieved July 2, 2006, from http://www.ntlf.com/html/lib/bib/writing.htm

Esch, C. (1998). Project-based and problem-based: Same or different? Retrieved July 7, 2006, from http://pblmm.k12.ca.us/PBLGuide/PBL&PBL.htm

Ferretti, R. P., MacArthur, C. D., & Okolo, C. M. (2001). Teaching for historical understanding in inclusive classrooms. *Learning Disability Quarterly, 24,* 59–71.

Fisher, D. (2005). The missing link: Standards, assessment, and instruction. *Voices from the Middle, 13*(2), 8–11.

Fisher, D., & Frey, N. (2003). Writing instruction for struggling adolescent readers: A gradual release model. *Journal of Adolescent and Adult Literacy, 46,* 396–407.

Fisher, D., & Frey, N. (2004). *Improving adolescent literacy: Strategies at work.* Upper Saddle River, NJ: Pearson/Merrill/Prentice Hall.

Fisher, D., & Frey, N. (2007). *Scaffolded writing: A gradual release approach to writing instruction.* New York: Scholastic.

Fisher, D., & Johnson, C. (2006). Using data to improve student achievement. *Principal Leadership, 7*(2), 27–31.

Fisher, D., Lapp, D., & Flood, J. (2005). Consensus scoring and peer planning: Meeting literacy accountability demands one school at a time. *The Reading Teacher, 58,* 656–667.

Flanders, N. (1970). *Analyzing teaching behavior.* Reading, MA: Addison-Wesley.

Flood, J., & Lapp, D. (1989). Reporting reading progress: A comparison portfolio for parents. *The Reading Teacher, 42,* 508–514.

Flynn, R. M. (2004). Curriculum-based Readers' Theatre: Setting the stage for reading and retention. *The Reading Teacher, 58*(4), 360–365.

Frey, N. (2003). A picture prompts a thousand words: Creating photo essays with struggling writers. *California English, 8*(5), 16–21.

Frey, N., & Fisher, D. (2006). *Language arts workshop: Purposeful reading and writing instruction.* Upper Saddle River, NJ: Pearson/Merrill/Prentice Hall.

Frey, N., & Fisher, D. (2007). *Reading for information in elementary school: Content literacy strategies to build comprehension.* Upper Saddle River, NJ: Pearson/Merrill/Prentice Hall.

Frey, N., Fisher, D., & Hernandez, T. (2003). What's the gist? Summary writing for struggling adolescent writers. *Voices from the Middle, 11*(2), 43–49.

Frey, N., & Hiebert, E. H. (2003). Teacher-based assessment of literacy learning. In J. Flood, D. Lapp, J. R. Squire, & J. Jensen (Eds.), *Handbook of research on teaching the English language arts* (2nd ed., pp. 608–618). Mahwah, NJ: Lawrence Erlbaum.

Fullan, M., Hill, P., & Crévola, C. (2006). *Breakthrough.* Thousand Oaks, CA: Corwin Press.

Gambrell, L., Koskinen, P. S., & Kapinus, B. A. (1991). Retelling and the reading comprehension of proficient and less-proficient readers. *Journal of Educational Research, 84,* 356–362.

Gardner, H. (1983). *Frames of mind: The theory of multiple intelligences.* New York: Basic Books.

Garthwait, A. (2004). Use of hypermedia in one middle school: A qualitative field study. *Journal of Educational Multimedia and Hypermedia, 13,* 219–243.

Ginsburg, H. (1982). *Children's arithmetic: The learning process* (Rev. ed.). New York: D. Van Nostrand.

Gollub, M. (2000). *The jazz fly.* Santa Rosa, CA: Tortuga Press.

Gonzalez, I. V. (1996). Third grade: Planning lessons for change and continuity. *Social Studies Review, 36*(1), 28–34.

Gould, L. L. (2001). *America in the Progressive Era, 1890–1914.* New York: Longman.

Gould, S. J. (1981). *The mismeasure of man.* New York: Norton.

Graves, D. H. (2002). *Testing is not teaching: What should count in education.* Portsmouth, NH: Heinemann.

Guan Eng Ho, D. (2005). Why do teachers ask the questions they ask? *RELC Journal, 36,* 297–310.

Hansen, J. (2004). *Tell me a story: Developmentally appropriate retelling strategies.* Newark, DE: International Reading Association.

Harvey, S., & Goudvis, A. (2000). *Strategies that work: Teaching comprehension to enhance understanding.* York, ME: Stenhouse.

Heward, W. L., Gardner, R., III, Cavanaugh, R. A., Courson, F. H., Grossi, T. A., & Barbetta, P. M. (1996). Everyone participates in this class: Using response cards to increase active student response. *Teaching Exceptional Children, 28*(2), 4–10.

Hmelo, C. (1998). Problem-based learning: Effects on early acquisition of cognitive skill in medicine. *The Journal of the Learning Sciences, 7,* 173–208.

Hobbs, R. (2001). Improving reading comprehension by using media literacy activities. *Voices from the Middle, 8*(4), 44–50.

Hofer, B. K., Yu, S. L., & Pintrich, P. R. (1998). Teaching college students to be self-regulated learners. In D. H. Schunk & B. J. Zimmerman (Eds.), *Self-regulated learning from teaching to self-reflective practice* (pp. 57–85). New York: Guilford.

Hopkinson, D. (1993). *Sweet Clara and the freedom quilt.* New York: Knopf.

Ivey, G., & Fisher, D. (2005). Learning from what doesn't work. *Educational Leadership, 63*(2), 8–17.

Johnson, D. W., & Johnson, R. (1998). Cooperative learning and social interdependence theory. In R. Tindale, L. Heath, J. Edwards, E. Posavac, F. Bryant, Y. Suzrez-Balcazar, et al. (Eds.), *Theory and research on small groups: Social psychological applications to social issues* (Vol. 4, pp. 9–36). New York: Plenum Press.

Johnson, D. W., & Johnson, R. T. (2002). *Meaningful assessment: A manageable and cooperative process.* Boston: Allyn and Bacon.

Joyce, B., & Showers, B. (2002). *Student achievement through staff development* (3rd ed.). Alexandria, VA: Association for Supervision and Curriculum Development.

Kagan, S. (1994). *Cooperative learning.* San Clemente, CA: Kagan Press.

Keys, C. W. (1999). Language as an indicator of meaning generation: An analysis of middle school students' written discourse about scientific investigations. *Journal of Research in Science Teaching, 36,* 1044–1061.

Kindsvatter, R., Wilen, W., & Ishler, M. (1996). *Dynamics of effective teaching* (3rd ed.). White Plains, NY: Longman.

Kirkland, L. D., & Patterson, J. (2005). Developing oral language in primary classrooms. *Early Childhood Education Journal, 32,* 391–395.

Kohn, A. (2000). *The case against standardized testing: Raising the scores, ruining the schools.* Portsmouth, NH: Heinemann.

Kooy, T. (1992). The effect of graphic advance organizers on math and science comprehension with high school special education students. *B.C. Journal of Special Education, 16*(2), 101–111.

Kotzwinkle, W., & Murray, G. (2001). *Walter, the farting dog.* New York: Dutton.

Kotzwinkle, W., & Murray, G. (2004). *Walter the farting dog: Trouble at the yard sale.* New York: Dutton.

Kotzwinkle, W., & Murray, G. (2005). *Walter the farting dog farts again.* New York: Dutton.

Kotzwinkle, W., Murray, G., & Gundy, E. (2005). *Rough weather ahead for Walter the farting dog.* New York: Dutton.

Kotzwinkle, W., Murray, G., & Gundy, E. (2006). *Walter the farting dog goes on a cruise.* New York: Dutton.

Koul, R., Clariana, R. B., & Salehi, R. (2005). Comparing several human and computer-based methods for scoring concept maps and essays. *Journal of Educational Computing Research, 32,* 227–239.

Kuhrt, B. L., & Farris, P. J. (1990). Empowering students through reading, writing, and reasoning. *Journal of Reading, 33,* 436–441.

Landorf, H., & Lowenstein, E. (2004). The Rosa Parks "myth": A third grade historical investigation. *Social Studies and the Young Learner, 16*(3), 5–9.

Langer, G. M., Colton, A. B., & Goff, L. S. (2003). *Collaborative analysis of student work: Improving teaching and learning.* Alexandria, VA: Association for Supervision and Curriculum Development.

Langer, J. A. (2001). Beating the odds: Teaching middle and high school students to read and write well. *American Educational Research Journal, 38,* 837–880.

Langley, A. (2005). *Ancient Egypt.* Chicago: Raintree.

Lapp, D., Fisher, D., Flood, J., & Cabello, A. (2001). An integrated approach to the teaching and assessment of language arts. In S. R. Hurley & J. V. Tinajero (Eds.), *Literacy assessment of second language learners* (pp. 1–26). Boston: Allyn and Bacon.

Lester, J. (1998). *From slave ship to Freedom Road.* New York: Dial Books.

Levine, M. G. (1995). Challenging limited English proficient history students with practical textbook activities. *Social Studies Review, 34*(2), 32–39.

Lingard, B., Hayes, D., & Mills, M. (2003). Teachers and productive pedagogies: Contextualising, conceptualising, utilising. *Pedagogy, Culture and Society, 11,* 399–424.

Linn, R. L., & Miller, M. D. (2005). *Measurement and assessment in teaching* (9th ed.). Upper Saddle River, NJ: Merrill Prentice Hall.

Lyman, F. T. (1981). The responsive classroom discussion: The inclusion of all students. In A. Anderson (Ed.), *Mainstreaming digest* (pp. 109–113). College Park, MD: University of Maryland Press.

Maccini, P., Gagnon, J. C., & Hughes, C. A. (2002). Technology-based practices for secondary students with learning disabilities. *Learning Disability Quarterly, 25,* 247–261.

MacDonald, S. (1997). *The portfolio and its use: A road map for assessment.* Little Rock, AR: Southern Early Childhood Association.

Maggi, A. (1999). Poetic stones: Roslin Chapel in Gandy's sketchbook and Daguerre's diorama. *Architectural History, 42,* 263–283.

Mandernach, B. J. (2003a). *Developing essay items.* [Online article]. Retrieved July 7, 2006, from www.park.edu/cetl/quicktips/essay.html

Mandernach, B. J. (2003b). *Developing short answer items.* [Online article]. Retrieved July 7, 2006, from www.park.edu/cetl/quicktips/shortanswer.html

Mandernach, B. J. (2003c). *Effective multiple-choice items.* [Online article]. Retrieved July 7, 2006, from www.park.edu/cetl/quicktips/multiple.html

Mandernach, B. J. (2003d). *Quality true–false items*. [Online article]. Retrieved July 7, 2006, from www.park.edu/cetl/quicktips/truefalse.html

Manzo, A. (1969). ReQuest: A method for improving reading comprehension through reciprocal questioning. *Journal of Reading, 12,* 123–126.

Marshall, J. (1974). *George and Martha*. New York: Houghton Mifflin.

Martinez, M., Roser, N. L., & Strecker, S. (1998–99). "I never thought I could be a star": A Readers' Theatre ticket to fluency. *The Reading Teacher, 52,* 326–334.

Marzano, R. J., Pickering, D. J., & Pollock, J. E. (2001). *Classroom instruction that works: Research-based strategies for increasing student achievement*. Alexandria, VA: Association for Supervision and Curriculum Development.

Mastropieri, M. A., Scruggs, T. E., & Graetz, J. E. (2003). Reading comprehension instruction for secondary students: Challenges for struggling students and teachers. *Learning Disability Quarterly, 26,* 103–116.

Mayer, R. E., & Gallini, J. K. (1990). When is an illustration worth ten thousand words? *Journal of Educational Psychology, 82,* 715–726.

McCarrier, A., Pinnell, G. S., & Fountas, I. C. (2000). *Interactive writing: How language and literacy come together, K–2*. Portsmouth, NH: Heinemann.

McCullen, C. (1997). Evaluating student presentations. Information Technology Evaluation Services, N. C. Department of Public Instruction. Retrieved February 7, 2007, from www.ncsu.edu/midlink/rub.pres.html

McDonald, N. (2005). Henri Matisse: Young readers' creative responses to the artist and his works. *The California Reader, 38*(4), 30–36.

McDonald, N., & Fisher, D. (2002). Strings attached: A musical listening unit. *Music Educators Journal, 88,* 32–38.

McKenna, M. C., & Robinson, R. D. (1980). *An introduction to the Cloze procedure: An annotated bibliography*. Newark, DE: International Reading Association.

Mertler, C. A. (2001). Designing scoring rubrics for your classroom. *Practical Assessment, Research and Evaluation, 7*(25), 1–10.

Meyer, D. K., Turner, J. C., & Spencer, C. A. (1997). Challenge in a mathematics classroom: Students' motivation and strategies in project-based learning. *The Elementary School Journal, 97,* 501–521.

Miller, L. D., & England, D. A. (1989). Writing to learn algebra. *School Science and Mathematics, 89,* 299–312.

Miller, S. L. (2006). Writing for learning and growth. Sonoma State University Writing Center. Retrieved February 7, 2007, from http://www.sonoma.edu/programs/writingcenter/pdf_files/assignmentsforlearning.pdf

MIT Online Writing and Communication Center. (1999). *Creating writing assignments*. Retrieved July 6, 2006, from http://web.mit.edu/writing/Faculty/createeffective.html

Monroe, E. E., & Pendergrass, M. R. (1997). Effects of mathematical vocabulary instruction on fourth grade students. *Reading Improvement, 34,* 120–132.

Moore, A., Sherwood, R., Bateman, H., Bransford, J. D., & Goldman, S. (1996, April). Using problem-based learning to prepare for project-based learning. Paper presented at the annual meeting of the American Educational Research Association, New York.

Moore, D. W., & Readence, J. E. (1984). A quantitative and qualitative review of graphic organizer research. *Journal of Educational Research, 78,* 11–17.

Morris, W. (1995). *My dog Skip*. New York: Random House.

National Center for Education Statistics. (2002). *More about NAEP writing*. [Online article]. Retrieved February 22, 2007, from http://nces.ed.gov/nationsreportcard/writing/moreabout.asp

National Research Council. (2000). *How people learn: Brain, mind, experience, and school.* J. D. Bransford, A. L. Brown, & R. R. Cocking (Eds.). Commission on Behavioral and Social Sciences and Education. Washington, DC: National Academy Press.

National Staff Development Council. (2001). *Standards for staff development* (Rev. ed.). Oxford, OH: Author.

Naylor, P. R. (1991). *Shiloh.* New York: Atheneum.

New Standards. (2001). *Speaking and listening for preschool through third grade.* Washington, DC: New Standards.

Ong, W. J. (1991). *Orality and literacy: The technologizing of the word.* New York: Routledge.

Orenstein, P. (1994). *Schoolgirls: Young women, self-esteem, and the confidence gap.* New York: Doubleday.

Ouaknin, M. A. (1999). *Mysteries of the alphabet: The origins of writing.* New York: Abbeville Press.

Oxley, D. (2005). *Smaller learning communities: Implementing and deepening practice.* Portland, OR: Northwest Regional Educational Laboratory.

Park, L. S. (2005). *Project Mulberry.* New York: Clarion.

Payne, R. K. (1995). *A framework: Understanding and working with students and adults from poverty.* Baytown, TX: RFT Publishing.

Persky, H. R., Daane, M. C., & Jin, Y. (2003). *The nation's report card: Writing 2002.* (NCES 2003529). Washington, DC: National Center for Education Statistics.

Podlozny, A. (2000). Strengthening verbal skills through the use of classroom drama: A clear link. *Journal of Aesthetic Education, 34*(3/4), 239–275.

Popham, W. J. (2003). Living (or dying) with your NCLB tests. *School Administrator, 60*(11), 10–14.

Radmacher, S. A., & Latosi-Sawin, E. (1995). Summary writing: A tool to improve student comprehension and writing in psychology. *Teaching of Psychology, 22,* 113–115.

Raphael, T. E., Highfield, K., & Au, K. H. (2006). *QAR now: Question answer relationships.* New York: Scholastic.

Rawls, W. (1961). *Where the red fern grows: The story of two dogs and a boy.* Garden City, NY: Doubleday.

Resnick, L. B. (2000). Making America smarter. *Education Week, 18*(40), 38–40.

Ringgold, F. (1992). *Aunt Harriet's Underground Railroad in the sky.* New York: Crown.

Ritchie, D., & Karge, B. D. (1996). Making information memorable: Enhanced knowledge retention and recall through the elaboration process. *Preventing School Failure, 41*(1), 28–33.

Romaine, S. (1994). *Language in society: An introduction to sociolinguistics.* New York: Oxford University Press.

Rothenberg, C., & Fisher, D. (2007). *Teaching English language learners: A differentiated approach.* Upper Saddle River, NJ: Pearson/Merrill/Prentice Hall.

Rowe, M. B. (1986). Wait-time: Slowing down may be a way of speeding up. *Journal of Teacher Education, 37*(1), 43–50.

Royer, R., & Royer, J. (2004). Comparing hand drawn and computer generated concept mapping. *Journal of Computers in Mathematics and Science Teaching, 23*(1), 67–81.

Sadker, M., & Sadker, D. (1986). Sexism in the classroom: From grade school to graduate school. *Phi Delta Kappan, 67,* 512–515.

Sadker, M., & Sadker, D. (1995). *Failing at fairness: How America's schools cheat girls.* New York: C. Scribner's Sons.

Sadker, M., Sadker, D., & Klein, S. (1991). The issue of gender in elementary and secondary education. In G. Grant (Ed.), *Review of research in education* (Vol. 17, pp. 269–334). Washington, DC: American Education Research Association.

Santa, C., & Havens, L. (1995). *Creating independence through student-owned strategies: Project CRISS.* Dubuque, IA: Kendall-Hunt.

Schauble, L. (1996). The development of scientific reasoning in knowledge-rich contexts. *Developmental Psychology, 32,* 102–119.

Schmoker, M. (2006). *Results now: How we can achieve unprecedented improvements in teaching and learning.* Alexandria, VA: Association for Supervision and Curriculum Development.

Schroeder, A. (1996). *Minty: A story of young Harriet Tubman.* New York: Dial Books for Young Readers.

Shanker, J. L., & Ekwall, E. E. (2003). *Locating and correcting reading difficulties* (8th ed.). Upper Saddle River, NJ: Merrill/Prentice Hall.

Shaughnessy, J. M. (1977). Misconceptions of probability: An experiment with a small-group, activity-based, model building approach to introductory probability at the college level. *Educational Studies in Mathematics, 8,* 295–316.

Shaw, D. (2005). *Retelling strategies to improve comprehension: Effective hands-on strategies for fiction and nonfiction that help students remember and understand what they read.* New York: Scholastic.

Shetterly, R. (2005). *Americans who tell the truth.* New York: Dutton Children's Books.

Short, D., & Echevarria, J. (2004/2005, December/January). Teacher skills to support English language learners. *Educational Leadership, 62*(4), 8–13.

Skillings, M. J., & Ferrell, R. (2000). Student-generated rubrics: Bringing students into the assessment process. *The Reading Teacher, 53,* 452–455.

Smith, R. C. (1920). Popular misconceptions in natural history. *The Scientific Monthly, 10*(2), 163–169.

Stabb, C. (1986). What happened to the sixth graders: Are elementary students losing their need to forecast and to reason? *Reading Psychology, 7,* 289–296.

Stein, R. C. (1997). *The Underground Railroad.* New York: Children's Press.

Stipek, D. (2004). Teaching practices in kindergarten and first grade: Different strokes for different folks. *Early Childhood Research Quarterly, 19,* 548–568.

Terman, L. M. (1916). *The measurement of intelligence: An explanation of and a complete guide for the use of the Standard revision and extension of the Binet-Simon intelligence scale.* Boston: Houghton Mifflin.

Tierney, R. J. (1998). Literacy assessment reform: Shifting beliefs, principled possibilities, and emerging practices. *The Reading Teacher, 51,* 374–390.

Tomlinson, C. A. (1999). *The differentiated classroom: Responding to the needs of all learners.* Alexandria, VA: Association for Supervision and Curriculum Development.

Tuckman, B. W. (1998). Using tests as an incentive to motivate procrastinators to study. *Journal of Experimental Education, 66*(2), 141–147.

van Langen, A., Bosker, R., & Dekkers, H. (2006). Exploring cross-national differences in gender gaps in education. *Educational Research and Evaluation, 12*(2), 155–177.

Vosniadou, S., Ioannides, C., Dimitrakopoulou, A., & Papademetriou, E. (2001). Designing learning environments to promote conceptual change in science. *Learning and Instruction, 11,* 381–419.

Walsh, J. A., & Sattes, B. D. (2005). *Quality questioning: Research-based practice to engage every learner.* Thousand Oaks, CA: Corwin Press.

Wang, C. (2000). How to grade essay examinations. *Performance Improvement, 39*(1), 12–15.

Wang, J. (2006, April). Developmental trends for badminton game play across skill levels: An exploratory study. Paper presented at the annual meeting of the American Education research Association, San Francisco, CA.

Webb, L. D. (2006). *The history of American education: A great American experiment.* Upper Saddle River, NJ: Pearson/Merrill/Prentice Hall.

Weiss, I., Kramarski, B., & Talis, S. (2006). Effects of multimedia environments on kindergarten children's mathematical achievements and style of learning. *Educational Media International, 43,* 3–17.

Wiggins, G. P., & McTighe, J. (1998). *Understanding by design.* Alexandria, VA: Association for Supervision and Curriculum Development.

Wiggins, G. P., & McTighe, J. (2005). *Understanding by design* (Expanded 2nd ed.). Alexandria, VA: Association for Supervision and Curriculum Development.

Wilcox, B. L. (1997). Writing portfolios: Active vs. passive. *English Journal, 86,* 34–37.

Wilhelm, J. D., & Smith, M. (2005). Asking the right questions: Literate lives of boys. *The Reading Teacher, 58,* 788–789.

Williams, J. P., Hall, K. M., Lauer, K. D., Stafford, K. B., DeSisto, L. A., & deCani, J. S. (2005). Expository text comprehension in the primary grade classroom. *Journal of Educational Psychology, 97,* 538–550.

Winerip, M. (2005, May 4). SAT essay test rewards length and ignores errors. *New York Times.* Retrieved July 6, 2006, from www.freerepublic.com/focus/f-news/1397024/posts

Winter, J. (1988). *Follow the drinking gourd.* New York: Knopf.

Wolf, D. (1987). Child development and different cognitive styles. *In Seminar proceedings: Issues in discipline-based art education: Strengthening the stage, extending the horizons* (pp. 3–8). Los Angeles: Getty Center for Education in the Arts.

Wong, H. K., & Wong, R. T. (2005). *First days of school: How to be an effective teacher.* Mountain View, CA: Author.

Wood, D., Bruner, J. S., & Ross, G. (1976). The role of tutoring in problem solving. *Journal of Psychology and Psychiatry, 17*(2), 89–100.

Wright, C. C. (1994). *Journey to freedom: A story of the Underground Railroad.* New York: Holiday House.

Yeh, S. S. (2005). Limiting the unintended consequences of high-stakes testing. *Education Policy Analysis Archives, 13*(43), 1–23

Zike, D. (1992). *Dinah Zike's big book of books and activities: An illustrated guide for teachers, parents, and anyone who works with kids!* San Antonio, TX: Dinah-Might Adventures.

Zike, D. (2004). *Dinah Zike's big book of science: Elementary K-6.* San Antonio, TX: Dinah-Might Adventures.

Zydney, J. M. (2005). Eighth-grade students defining complex problems: The effectiveness of scaffolding in a multimedia program. *Journal of Educational Multimedia and Hypermedia, 14,* 61–90.

Index

Note: Page references for figures are indicated with an *f* after the page numbers.

About the Authors

Douglas Fisher, PhD, is a professor of language and literacy education in the Department of Teacher Education at San Diego State University (SDSU), the codirector for the Center for the Advancement of Reading at the California State University Chancellor's Office, and a past director of professional development for the City Heights Educational Collaborative. He is the recipient of the International Reading Association Celebrate Literacy Award as well as the Christa McAuliffe award for excellence in teacher education from the American Association of State Colleges and Universities. He has published numerous articles on reading and literacy, differentiated instruction, and curriculum design as well as books, including *Creating Literacy-Rich Schools for Adolescents* (with Gay Ivey), *Improving Adolescent Literacy: Strategies at Work* (with Nancy Frey), and *Teaching English Language Learners: A Differentiated Approach* (with Carol Rothenberg). Doug has taught a variety of courses in SDSU's teacher-credentialing program as well as graduate-level courses on English language development and literacy. A former early intervention specialist and language development specialist, he has also taught high school English, writing, and literacy development to public school students. He can be reached at dfisher@mail.sdsu.edu.

Nancy Frey, PhD, is an associate professor of literacy in the School of Teacher Education at San Diego State University. Before joining the university faculty, Nancy was a teacher in the Broward County (Florida) Public Schools, where she taught both general and special education students at the elementary and middle school levels. She later worked for the Florida Department of Education on a statewide project for supporting students with diverse learning needs in general education curriculum. She is also a recipient of the Christa McAuliffe award for excellence in teacher education. Her research interests include reading and literacy, assessment, intervention, and curriculum design. She has coauthored several books on literacy, including *Language Arts Workshop: Purposeful Reading and Writing Instruction* and *Reading for Information in Elementary School* (both with Doug Fisher). She teaches a variety of courses in SDSU's teacher-credentialing program on elementary and secondary literacy in content-area instruction and supporting students with diverse learning needs. She can be reached at nfrey@mail.sdsu.edu.

Related ASCD Resources: Formative Assessment

At the time of publication, the following ASCD resources were available; for the most up-to-date information about ASCD resources, go to www.ascd.org. ASCD stock numbers are noted in parentheses.

Audio

Differentiated Instruction: The Complex Issue of Academically Diverse Classrooms by Carol Ann Tomlinson (Audiotape: #203173; CD: #503266)

Increasing Student Responsibility for Learning Through Active Engagement and Critical Partnerships by Judy Ness (Audiotape: #204076; CD: #504110)

Understanding by Design and Differentiated Instruction: Partners in Classroom Success by Grant Wiggins, Jay McTighe, and Carol Ann Tomlinson (Audiotape: #203188; CD: #503281)

Mixed Media

Formative Assessment Strategies For Every Classroom—An ASCD Action Tool (three-ring binder, 245 pages) by Susan Brookhart (#707010)

Networks

Visit the ASCD Web site (www.ascd.org) and click on About ASCD and then on Networks for information about professional educators who have formed groups around topics, including "Assessment for Learning." Look in the "Network Directory" for current facilitators' addresses and phone numbers.

Print Products

Classroom Assessment and Grading That Works by Robert Marzano (#106006)

The Differentiated Classroom: Responding to the Needs of All Learners by Carol Ann Tomlinson (#199040)

Educational Leadership, February 1994: Teaching for Understanding (Entire Issue #194025)

Educational Leadership, November 2005: Assessment to Promote Learning (Entire Issue #106038)

Enhancing Professional Practice: A Framework for Teaching, 2nd Edition by Charlotte Danielson (#106034)

Enhancing Student Achievement: A Framework for School Improvement by Charlotte Danielson (#102109)

Integrating Differentiated Instruction and Understanding by Design: Connecting Content and Kids by Carol Ann Tomlinson and Jay McTighe (#105004)

Understanding by Design, Expanded 2nd Edition by Grant Wiggins and Jay McTighe (#103055)

Understanding by Design Professional Development Workbook by Jay McTighe and Grant Wiggins (#103056)

Videos and DVDs

At Work in the Differentiated Classroom (three 28- to 48-minute programs on DVD and a 195-page facilitator's guide) (# 601071)

Moving Forward with Understanding by Design (one 75-minute DVD with a comprehensive user guide) (#607012)

Understanding by Design (three 25- to 55-minute programs on one DVD) (#600241)

A Visit to a Differentiated Classroom (one 60-minute videotape with an online viewer's guide) (#401309)

For additional resources, visit us on the World Wide Web (http://www.ascd.org), send an e-mail message to member@ascd.org, call the ASCD Service Center (1-800-933-ASCD or 703-578-9600, then press 2), send a fax to 703-575-5400, or write to Information Services, ASCD, 1703 N. Beauregard St., Alexandria, VA 22311-1714 USA.